The Church and Family

J.D. Middlebrook
Larry Summers

GOSPEL PUBLISHING HOUSE
SPRINGFIELD, MISSOURI

02-0482

© 1980 by the Gospel Publishing House, Springfield,
Missouri 65802. This is a Workers Training Division textbook.
Sunday School Department, Assemblies of God.
Library of Congress Catalog Card Number 80-66326
International Standard Book Number 0-88243-482-9
Printed in the United States of America

Introduction

ON JULY 15, 1979, PRESIDENT JIMMY CARTER addressed the American public with an assertion of a need for moral and family values in a speech known as "The Crisis of Confidence." The American people responded to this emphasis on the needs of the American family with more than 100,000 pieces of mail—overwhelmingly positive. As a result, a few months later in Kansas City, Missouri, the president announced the establishment of an "Office for Families" in the Department of Health, Education, and Welfare.

Christian leaders everywhere are spending more and more of their time attempting to counsel and heal hurting families—which is commendable. However, they should concentrate the greater portion of their time and energies developing enrichment rather than remedial ministries.

The concept that we can do something positive within families through planned change is relatively new—emotionally, cognitively, and socially. There has been some resistance to planned change due to the fact that families have no cultural methods of checking on themselves and their interaction, and sometimes it is felt that admitting the need for help is a sign of weakness.

There may be continued resistance to change because family life is private and isolated in our culture, and parents often feel they should be able to work out their own difficulties. The mystique that Christian families should not have problems may also cause further resistance to change in the Sunday school and church.

In this book, we are concerned with understanding God's design for the family and establishing Biblical structures and functions that will prevent the family from having problems. At the same time, we recognize that even among born-again Christians there are adjustments and differences and it is necessary to overcome the attitude of our times that has made the disintegration of the family one of the greatest challenges of the church.

The authors realize they cannot give a comprehensive perspective on the family in this book. Instead, they have attempted to promote a commitment to family-enrichment ministry from Christian leaders and teachers. Family enrichment is the process of enriching or deepening the strengths and attributes a family *already* has in order to provide growth and fulfillment for the family members, as well as the family as a whole.

Both the church and Sunday school have an equal responsibility to give themselves to family nurture and enrichment. Hopefully, when a church implements this study, ideas will be conveyed that will help the family survive with a Biblical pattern and become stronger.

Virginia Satir said:

When families become as important to America as football or firearms, the divorce rate will take a deep plunge, nonreaders will cease to become a national problem, juvenile delinquency will experience dropouts, and neighborhoods will once again become a place for people of all ages to live together.

Contents

1

The Biblical Foundations
for Family Life

YOU AND I ARE PART OF A FAMILY. We have no choice. It is by design that God has made the family the basic unit of all society. The family was God's idea, and the ideal for His Christian family is set forth in various scriptural pictures in the Word of God.

Aggressive anti-family sentiments are being expressed by some in our day, even suggesting to love family life and believe it is of paramount importance is a heretic's position.

If this is indeed true, then I confess to being a heretic, for I am convinced as I study the Word of God that God's idea of the family is the answer for the emotional, spiritual, psychological, and social needs of each human being.

Admittedly today, the distinctively Christian family seems to be passing out of existence by default. The family as traditionally perceived is in trouble. It takes time to make a house a home and often we do not take the time that is necessary to establish the Christian home and family. It is hoped that every Sunday school worker, every parent, and every child will be inspired to a new and determined effort to implement the Biblical pattern for building a strong family life.

Contrary to common thought, one does not have a Christian home simply because everyone in the home is a professed Christian. This is where so many fail to understand and establish a truly Christian home and family life. It is not a trite observation to suggest that this nation has been made great and strong from its inception because of the moral and spiritual fiber of the Christian home. What is making this nation bankrupt today and corrupt within is the breakdown of the home, particularly the Christian home, and the departure from Biblical principles by society in general.

7

There are other institutions in society for the benefit of mankind, but the single most important factor in molding and socializing human beings is the family. It will either prepare the child to reach ultimate fulfillment or cripple and inhibit him from achieving his potential. When a society fails to give proper place to family life it suffers irreparable loss, and history indicates that ancient civilizations failed because of a disregard for the family.

The first institution was the family. God established certain institutions as basic building blocks for a solid and safe social order. We will look at these so we may understand God's idea.

In the beginning God endowed man with volition or free will. Then, God established three institutions. First He established marriage. Second, He established the family. And third, He established human government. In the New Testament He established the Christian church to support these three institutions and to give guidance to man's "will," that he might choose right.

God in His wisdom designed man with a "will," that he might choose for himself the right or the wrong way to live (Genesis 2:15-17). Whichever way man chooses, he becomes responsible for his choice and is held accountable by his Creator. This is an awesome reality, but privileges imply responsibilities. In the New Testament we are told, "Every man shall give an account." God, with all His sovereignty, will not violate man's free will. He gives instructions and directions so man may choose the right and forsake the wrong.

With regard to family life and understanding our responsibility as family leaders, family members, and Christian educators, we must teach so this "will" may be exercised in the proper direction, that right choices may be made. If we choose wrong we are responsible to our Creator (Deuteronomy 11:26-28).

"As goes the home, so goes the nation,
As goes the marriage, so goes the home,
As goes the individual, so goes the marriage."
(Source Unknown)

Accepting our responsibility is fundamental. Let us learn this truth and teach it to others. We must not blame others for our failures, but seek to make the right choices. Failures in the past are not final. The wonderful truth is: "It is of the Lord's mercies . . . his compassions fail not. They are new every morning" (Lamentations 3:22, 23).

Marriage Was God's Idea (Genesis 2:21-24, *NASB*)

Marriage is the greatest of human relationships and is taught throughout the Bible. God's Word is the greatest teacher of monogamy, the union of one man and one woman. God enters into this marriage contract and He will keep His part. When He brings a man and a woman into this contractual relationship it is with a view to permanence. God's covenants are faithful and consistent and this is the way He ordained marriage to be.

Yes, there are violations of this rule, but such cases are to be regarded as contrary to the underlying principle of marriage. This is not to suggest any other family structure can never know God's blessings, but He established the pattern of the union of one man and one woman.

Genesis 3 records the fall of man but this occurred after God's creative provision for marriage and sex and was in no way responsible for the Fall, as is erroneously taught by some. A great need on the American scene is for Christian educators to focus on the Biblical concept of marriage.

A marriage bond involves one man and one woman, these two alone, joined together to become "one flesh." The Scriptures teach us in Hebrews 13:4: "Marriage is honorable in all." Anyone who comes in as a third party and breaks this unit that God has established must deal with the Creator himself; God will be their judge. And anyone who allows a third party to come in will also be judged (Matthew 19:6).

In His teaching, Jesus reaffirmed the permanence of the marital relationship. Genesis 2:23, 24 has been called the great "charter of monogamy," and Jesus quoted it when He explained the marriage relationship: "They twain shall be one flesh." The "two become one." As Jesus said: "Wherefore they are no more twain, but one flesh" (Matthew 19:6). Nothing but death separates a man from his own flesh.

The Family Is Established

God established a foundation of family life when He spoke to

Israel and ultimately to all mankind. In Deuteronomy 6, He talks of the "statutes and commandments" and, in verse 7 how to meet the challenges of family life.

It will be agreed that parents and children must experience life and learn and grow together. However, we are not only concerned with the development of conscience and character, but also with the "communication of faith" as a vital and living relationship with God. This involves the totality of our personality—our values, attitudes, beliefs, and behavior. To communicate such faith from generation to generation, a deep and loving togetherness is absolutely essential.

Scripture focuses on certain responsibilities, and in Deuteronomy God gives Israel some very practical and vital directions. I am indebted to Dr. Ray Brock for calling these principles to my attention.

First, these truths are to be taught "when you sit in your house" (6:7, *NASB*). For most of us, the one time we sit down together is at the dinner hour. Our rapid pattern of life robs us of much togetherness, but the dinner hour can be "our family time." It should not be a time when problems or discipline are discussed, but time for sharing our faith in our homes. Listen for any needs that may be expressed and be careful not to allow distractions, such as arguments or TV watching. Let family life be cultivated at the dinner table.

Second, these truths are to be taught "when you walk by the way." This speaks of productivity. All children should be taught the basic techniques of survival in our culture. It is not fair for a mother to do all the duties around the home. Both the girls and the boys should learn. It is not fair for the father to care for all the duties of his role around the house. In all these things we should share with our family, and while we work together we must keep in mind the ultimate goal is to share our faith, for the "communication of faith is a family affair."

Third, these truths are to be taught "when you lie down." Evening brings "talk time." I remember when my daughters were growing up, in the quietness of the evening, at their prayer time, they were willing to talk about their concerns. It is important for fathers to be involved in the time when the children lie down. They need to hold, cuddle, bathe, and tuck them in and to hear their prayers. The Christian faith and family life are not only a mother's responsibility; they are also the father's. Parents should share their faith at the time of lying down.

Fourth, these truths are to be taught "when you rise up." We teach much and determine much about our attitude toward life when we rise up in the morning. We need to approach each day with excitement. It is a day the Lord has given us. We face our mission with Him. And we need to convey this to our children and share our faith with them.

Ephesians 5:21 through 6:4 speaks of the responsibilities of the husband and wife, each toward the other; of the children toward their parents; and, particularly, of the father's role in discipline and sharing the faith in the home. A striking point is made in Ephesians 6:4: "Fathers, do not provoke your children to anger; but bring them up in the discipline and instruction of the Lord" *(NASB)*.

We will speak later about the role of the father, but I would like to emphasize that although a man may be a Christian, he may still not be properly adjusted in his relationship with his family. When a man is a tyrant, the children will usually rebel against the position and faith of the father. When a father is only a tenant in his home and someone else is running the show, the children will go their own way. If they turn out right, it will be in spite of their home training and they will have a warped idea of what Christian family life is really like. The father's ideal role is that of a tutor, training his household in the things of the Lord and in living the Christian life.

One of the most tragic errors is to believe we can be "smiles and sunshine" at church and with others, but fail in living the Christian life when no one but the family is around. It's possible to fool the pastor and other people but we'll never fool our children. They see through us and will rebel against the empty hypocritical profession of either the father or the mother.

The home is never the *last* place to live the Christian life; it is always the *first* place. Family life was established by God in the beginning of human history, and it should be a priority with His people.

Government Is Established

After the flood of Noah's day, God instituted human government as a controlling influence over vice and corruption in society (Genesis 9). It was for the purpose of protecting man from those depraved individuals who hadn't learned socialization in their family or had refused to obey God's principles regarding others and their property. The highest power of human government is the taking of a man's life. This power of government necessitates and establishes all lesser powers for controlling lawlessness. Government, Paul observes in Romans 13, is not conceived by man but ordained by God.

The Church Is Established

Tim and Beverly LaHaye have noted in *Spirit-Controlled Family Living* (Old Tappan, NJ: Fleming H. Revell, 1978):

> Whenever the church has done her work positively she has so strengthened her families that they have served as a stabilizing influence in society, producing freedom, liberty, and opportunity unequalled in any of the pagan cultures of the world. When the church has failed in her teaching role it has been at the expense of both family and society.

The church was established many centuries after the family and government, and it supports the family. We, as leaders in the church and fellow members of the body of Christ, have a concern for family life. For, if the family is strong then the church is strong. Sunday school teachers must realize the Sunday school does not replace the home but is a support system for the family and the home. We have a duty to nurture and equip individuals and families for growth and effective functioning.

Lawrence O. Richards, at the Continental Congress on the Family (St. Louis, 1975), noted:

> The notion that husband, wife, and children are a complete unit without need for support from without is one of the romanticized fictions of secular society; it is not Biblical.

The home and church are not in competition but are intended to be mutually supportive.

We in the church must not follow secular society and abdicate our responsibility and allow the Christian family to pass out of existence by default. Let us note some trends in the church that make the situation hopeful. For example, there is a recognition that the communication of faith is a family affair. There is a trend toward making the home the center for nurture. There are family-life programs, and many of our churches have noted what God is doing in bringing new attention to the family. The family as a unit and family members in particular will find help in this new concern.

The Ten Commandments

The Ten Commandments are a succinct summary of the moral relationships and duties of man to God and to others. They give insight into God's concern for man's well-being. The first four commandments pertain to our relationship to God, while the following six concern human relationships. Of these six, three pertain to the family.

Commandments are not given to people who are ignorant of the subject to which they relate. It would be absurd to give a commandment regarding an unknown moral relationship. From the beginning, man has innately understood the need for family.

The first of the three commandments relating to the family is the fifth commandment: "Honor thy father and thy mother" (Exodus 20:12; Deuteronomy 5:16). This obviously refers to the relation of children to parents. This commandment could scarcely have arisen when polygamy was a common practice, and certainly never from promiscuity. The equality of father and mother is apparent; honor is to be given to both.

The seventh commandment: "Thou shalt not commit adultery" (Exodus 20:14; Deuteronomy 5:18), secures the home. It says that whatever children are born to the race shall be born in a home and of that home; that is, they shall be "family born."

All or any sexual union outside marriage is barred. Outside the family, sexual union is sin. The family is the primal and oldest institution of man; the greatest and the holiest. Over this institution the seventh commandment stands as a sentry.

The 10th commandment seems almost out of place among the others (Exodus 20:17; Deuteronomy 5:21). They all enjoin specific acts. The 10th seems to foreshadow the Saviour's teaching; dealing with the thoughts and intents of the heart. It is an attempt at regulation *within* man. It goes beyond outward acts and deals with the spirit.

While this commandment seems to apply primarily to the rights of property, it lists the things most common to family life—house, servant, animal. One is forbidden not only "to take" but also to desire such things. In the list of things belonging to a neighbor that a man is forbidden to desire, the term *wife* is included. It may seem strange that she should be listed along with property. One of woman's greatest blessings to man is helpfulness. Eve was the mother of all living and a helpmeet for Adam. Sarah was the mistress of domestic operation. A wife who is quick of thought, accurate in judgment, and deft of hand is usually the key to a man's material prosperity.

It is well to remember that half of the commandments pertaining to human relationships hold the family plainly in view. This helps us to understand the high priority God places on the family.

The Biblical Roles for Members of the Family

There is a great deal of role confusion in today's world. We will speak to this as one of the issues facing the family, but first let us look at the Biblical directions for family roles. Teachers of Christian education classes would do well to study these Biblical patterns so they may be properly discussed and understood in the classroom.

The Roles of the Husband

It has never been easy to be a good husband, anymore than it is easy to be a good Christian. It takes effort, but help and direction are available in the Word of God.

First, the husband is to be the *leader and head* of his family: "For the husband is the head of the wife, even as Christ is the head of the church: and he is the saviour of the body" (Ephesians 5:23). God clearly defined the relationship in Genesis 3:16: "And thy desire shall be to thy husband, and he shall rule over you." This principle is stated again and again in the Word of God. Male leadership should be respected by all members of the family. The husband is a servant as a leader, just as Christ is Head of the Church. It is a *leadership* of love.

The husband is to be an ideal *lover*. Ephesians 5:25 states that he is to love his wife as Christ loved the Church. And he is told to love his neighbor "as himself." It is a sacrificial kind of love that the Bible speaks of. Love that is given shall be happily returned. Study again 1 Corinthians 13:4-8 for the characteristics of Biblical love. Love is certainly a feeling and a motivator, but it is also a command of the Scriptures.

The husband is to be the family *provider*. God laid this down in Genesis 3:19: "In the sweat of thy face shall thou eat bread." Man has been accountable for both the financial provision and the psychological and physical protection of his family throughout the Scriptures. Paul laid the responsibility heavily on the man in 1 Timothy 5:8: "But if any provide not . . . for those of his own house, he hath denied the faith, and is worse than an infidel."

The husband is the primary *breadwinner* for the family. He is the *protector* not only from physical evils but also from emotional and spiritual hurts. The husband is a *father-teacher*. Psalm 127:3 teaches: "Lo, children are a heritage of the Lord." If God has given us children, we will be accountable for them. Being a good father takes work, sacrifice, and time, but there are built-in blessings from being faithful in this area.

Fathers are to *love* their children: "Provoke not your children to wrath" (Ephesians 6:4). Children need love from their father, as well as *teaching*: "Fathers, . . . bring them [your children] up in the nurture and admonition of the Lord." We are to train them by example and precept in the ways of our God. Children are to be disciplined, for self-discipline, self-control, and self-denial are essential in maturing to adulthood.

The father is to be the *priest* of his house. He should teach his children love for the Word of God, the importance of prayer, and faithfulness to the house of God and the things of God. He will teach his children stewardship by the example of his own life.

Roles of the Wife

Again the Bible is very clear as to the roles of the wife. Her career is to be a magnificent one.

First, she is to be a *helpmeet* (Genesis 2). Ephesians 5:22 says: "Wives, be subject to your own husbands" *(NASB)*. There is a rejection of this submission by many modern women.

Usually it is because they do not understand what the Bible teaches. Subjection or *submission* does not mean suppression or silence. It does not make Christian women second-rate citizens any more than Christ was second-rate because He assumed a place of subjection and was in a supportive role to God the Father in the Godhead. Submission is reserved "unto your own husband."

Study again 1 Peter 3:1, 2:

In the same way, you wives, be submissive to your own husbands so that even if any of them are disobedient to the word, they may be won without a word by the behavior of their wives, as they observe your chaste and respectful behavior (*NASB*).

Second, the wife should be the *home manager*. This is her kingdom, her realm. No woman should ever say, "I am just a homemaker." What a wonderful privilege God has given the lady of the house to manage, under God, her home. Attitudes are very important. Study again Proverbs 31:10-31. (In the book *Spirit-Controlled Family Living* by Tim and Beverly LaHaye, there is a 20th-century portrayal of the woman in Proverbs which gives insight into the modern application of this passage. It would be worthy of your study.)

The woman of the family is to be the *lover*. A wife need not be afraid to enjoy the intimacy of the act of marriage, for this was the design and plan of God:

Let the husband fulfill his duty toward his wife, and likewise also the wife to her husband. The wife does not have authority over her own body, but the husband does; likewise also the husband does not have authority over his own body, but the wife does (1 Corinthians 7:3, 4, *NASB*).

Love can be nurtured and developed and it ought to be.

The wife is a *mother-teacher* in the home. When a mother is delighted with "a gift from God" and desires to mold the life of this child as pleasing to the Lord, motherhood will be a joy to her. A primary responsibility is toward her children.

The Role of the Parent

To be a parent is both a privilege and a responsibility. Couples should plan to be responsible parents; serving, under

God, as ministers to their children. Many of today's problems could be resolved if we saw our role as parents as a ministry.

The birth of every child should be planned and desired by both parents. Children should not be used to satisfy our own selfishness. Parents are co-workers with God in creation. The purpose of God is that parents plan for children, then in the fulfillment of their marriage union bring a child to Him. In a special way, parent-love centered in a child is a fulfillment.

Parenthood begins with the child's birth and continues throughout his life. In the family, God intends children to be nurtured and to mature. Parents are responsible for the whole environment of their children.

Couples who are childless might prayerfully consider adoption. Highlands Child Placement Service of the Assemblies of God can give counsel and help.

Parents must accept the fact that well-adjusted children are seldom found where there are maladjusted parents. Harmony in marriage is our responsibility so our children's emotional needs, such as security, will be met.

When we take our role seriously and prayerfully, God helps us in one of life's great privileges—being a parent.

Summary

The Bible gives us insight as to God's plan for the human family. It is to be monogamous, Christian, and law-obeying, with the father and mother having responsible roles and the children maturing in a protected, wholesome environment.

Discussion Activities

1. The family is basic to a well-ordered society.
2. Man's well-being is dependent on God-ordained institutions. Explain how they fit into God's plan.
3. How do you understand the concept of "roles"?
4. Write a half-page description of your role in your family. Discuss it with other family members.
5. Teachers in the Sunday school can strengthen the family by giving attention to the Biblical principles.

2
The Family Today

THERE ARE MANY INTERESTING PROFILES that have been done on the current status of the American family. Various reports are to be found in newspapers and magazines. For example, in the *Greenville Piedmont* (South Carolina), June 27, 1979, it was reported:

The number of unmarried couples living together has more than doubled in less than a decade, accounting for about 1.1 million U.S. households, the census bureau said. . . .

Meanwhile, more than 20 percent of all households have only a single member, as increasing numbers of young career-oriented Americans postpone marriage. . . .

Among unmarried couples, seven out of ten were under the age of 45. [One-fourth of these couples have children living with them.]

In August 1979, the Religious News Service reported that nearly one of every five American children now lives in a one-parent household, compared to about 1 in 10 in 1960. During the same period the number of single-parent families headed by women increased by 131 percent!

Among other factors reported by the U.S. Census Bureau was a 1978 divorce rate of 5.1 per 1,000 marriages. This means about 4 marriages in every 10 will end in divorce if that 1-year rate continues. The number of children involved in divorce has increased from 361,000 to 1,117,000 in the 20-year period between 1956 and 1976.

Threats to the Christian Family

There are many threats in modern life to the family. I think

19

one of the tragic misconceptions of family life is that the normal family does not experience problems, conflicts, and stress. This myth seems to persist especially in the church where it is assumed that Christian families should live in perfect peace and harmony. However, every significant study of the family demonstrates the normal family does not always live in perfect harmony. It does at times have conflicts and there are periods when cooperation among its members simply does not exist. The difference between the healthy family and the destructive family is not a lack of problems, but rather how these problems are viewed, conceptualized, and finally confronted.

If you categorized all the challenges a family might face, they might be organized into two groups, according to Dr. Kenneth Chafin in his book *Is There a Family in the House* (Waco, TX: Word Books, 1978). The first group would be those problems that grow out of the normal living of a family as it moves from marriage to parenthood, to the departure of the children from the home, and finally to retirement for the couple. Each stage has its own problems which, at the same time, give opportunities for growth. The second set of problems is not due to the family itself, but come from the society of which the family is an integral part. No one will deny the social pressures on the family these days.

There are rapid changes created by an age of technology never before encountered in human history. There is a pluralization of society, and the functions once assigned to the family are now distributed to other units of society. Add to this the advocates of social change and the critics who have urged the overthrow of Christian morality, and there is a serious "values and morals" problem. It is not uncommon to learn of college students being counseled to "live together until it's practical to marry."

The women's lib extremists cry "equality" and urge women to get out of their homes and exercise their rights; telling them fulfillment can never be found in the home.

Drug abuse continues to be a problem, reaching into the elementary and junior high schools and damaging our whole society. There are now an estimated 450,000 child alcoholics in our nation. Promiscuity is increasing and in some schools pregnancy is seen as a status symbol. It has been estimated that one-half of the brides under 19 are pregnant. Violence has become commonplace. No influence is greater in bringing all the pressures of society to bear on the family than the various media, particularly television.

The Media and the Family

At one time many people considered all media to be amoral—neither good nor bad. Then there was a period when any new medium, such as radio and then television, was essentially immoral. The truth is one of the great responsibilities of the Christian home is to monitor and regulate the media. Whether a TV show is a news program, a documentary, or a comedy, the medium tends to make fantasy seem real and reality seem like fiction. This is why it is such a threat.

In America, 95 percent of the homes have televisions and, in 1978, the average home spent 5¾ hours daily watching TV. Commercials convey the idea that happiness depends on what we buy. Of each hour, 16 minutes are given to advertising. Five of the most advertised products for children's shows are cereal, snack foods, and candy, which are now being viewed as detrimental to the nutritional well-being of children.

The political influence of television is seen in that John Kennedy won the Presidency of the United States because of his television appearances. The news media has a tremendous influence. All national news is filtered through one group of men in one city, New York City. There are four major cities that are sources of news: New York, Chicago, Los Angeles, and Washington, D.C. The general view is that "news is what is reported; what is not reported is not news."

Violence is such a part of television that by the time a child turns 12, he has viewed 101,000 violent episodes. The general message conveyed is that money and wealth are the ultimate goals in life, and violence is okay if you are on the right side. It is a documented fact that children are developing a tolerance for violence in America at an unprecedented pace.

I read a release from the Population Crisis Committee for the year 1979. It reported that 40 million women had abortions; representing one-fourth of all pregnancies worldwide. Abortions in the United States, Canada, and most western European countries, tended to be among women in their twenties or younger and often they were unmarried. Abortion has become a horrible threat to Christian morality.

Human sexuality is being discussed more openly than ever before. Some of this openness contributes to the well-being of the family, but some is detrimental. Those who have placed human sexuality on the animal level have degraded one of the noblest creative gifts of God within the framework of marriage. God said, "The marriage bed is undefiled." But, contrary to God's design, sexuality has been viewed by the modern mind as an end in itself.

Role confusion also threatens the family, and marriage itself is being viewed as an outmoded concept. Some are asking: "Is marriage an outdated idea?" And some of those who still advocate marriage suggest a "contractual marriage" that is renewed periodically or dissolved at the end of the contract.

Society surrounds your family and mine with tremendous pressures. The family is a social institution. We are part of our society; it influences us and we ought to influence society. In spite of the threats and radical changes it is experiencing, by God's wondrous grace the Christian family will survive, although some of its functions may change. How a family will meet the challenges will depend on how it views: the family's importance, the Biblical foundations for establishing the family, and the marital relationship of the husband and wife and their roles. Their understanding of these things will determine the kind of family life they will have and the persons they will be.

The Functions of the Family

In our role as parents, only as we function in a Biblical manner do we make our society strong and strengthen other institutions, such as the church and the government.

Sociologists have long defined certain functions of the family. Without comment we will simply list these:

1. Procreation or reproduction.
2. Regulation of sexual needs.
3. Protection of the young born to this union.
4. The conferring of status by occupation and defined right of interaction.

5. Affection; that is, the giving and receiving of love.
6. A stabilizing effect by providing an anchor in society.
7. Economic function; that is, consumer and production function.
8. Educational or socialization function; that is, the teaching of values and how to live in relationship to others.
9. The function of religious training.
10. The governing function or discipline.
11. The recreation or leisure function.
12. The care of the aged and the ill.

Hopefully, in the Christian family the greatest influence on the child—more than the school, the church, or the government—is the home. Christians, therefore, should recognize their responsibility to nurture and teach their children. A Christian home is where spiritual life can *begin*. A Christian home is where spiritual life can be *nurtured* (Ephesians 6:4). A Christian home is where a child can gain the self-confidence he needs to successfully deal with an unfriendly world.

The Church and the Family

The church exists to minister. One of the focuses of this ministry must be the family. The church is a support system to nurture and equip individuals and families for growth and effective functioning. The family is not meant to be a self-contained system. Family members need the support of a local body of believers. In today's world, it is even more vital that families receive support from the church.

What are the supporting roles for the body of believers to the family?

1. The church must accept the responsibility to minister to and support believers as families and to help individuals fulfill vital family roles. This can be a challenge to the teacher of any age-group—from the smallest child to the oldest member of the Sunday school.
2. Ministry should avoid a "program approach" and involve members in a two-way ebb and flow of ministry in interpersonal settings. A series of sermons on the family does not

meet this function. There must be interaction of all ages within the church body.

3. There should be support of families as units to develop a "relational climate" that makes possible the two-way flow of ministry within each family.

4. The church should help individual family members understand how to fulfill their divinely ordained roles. For example, Paul wrote in Titus 2:3-5 that the widows should minister to the young wives and teach them how to love their husbands and children.

Husbands need to understand their roles, and parents need to learn how to guide their children and exercise authority constructively. The role-reversal problem that is a factor in homosexual development occurs in the home without a Biblical structure.

5. The body of believers can help other believers develop distinctive Christian life-styles, expressed in Christian living. A life-style is not developed by verbalizing ideas alone. It requires socialization; the sharing of a total way of living. This encompasses beliefs, values, attitudes, emotions, and behavior. (Deuteronomy 6:6-9 deals with this theme.)

There is much confusion about what is a Christian family. Some suppose a Christian family is one in which all the members are Christians. But this is a simplistic view. A Christian family is a family that has learned to handle its conflicts in a Biblical manner, has developed a life-style compatible with the New Testament church, and has learned a pattern of Christian values which it is communicating within the family. When a commitment is made to Christ's kingdom, there is suffering and happiness, sacrifice and blessing.

In a Christian family there must be both formal and informal teaching. I shall be forever indebted to my parents who read the Bible and practiced its teachings and took me with them to Sunday school and church. I learned early to value the church and its place in family life. My parents showed me the worth of Spirit-filled Christian living in everyday situations. I shared in a strong Christian family and my life was directed Godward by that experience.

Teachers in our Christian education programs must see

themselves as partners with parents in communicating Christian values. These values must not be in word only, but also in the life-style of the teacher and other leaders. There must be honesty and openness on the part of those within the family as well as those in the church. Teachers may teach the importance of church, and that is good, but they must also be available when their students need them.

Spiritual Development and the Home

Dr. Ted Ward, of Michigan State University, has given the following distinctive values of the Christian family (*All Church News Service*):

1. The sanctity of and commitment to the marriage relationship.
2. The home as a place of warmth, nurture, acceptance, and healthy stimulation.
3. Growth in grace and the knowledge of God as a family and as individuals, through the Bible and its implementation in a just, merciful, and loving life-style.
4. Involvement in outreach, through the church; participating in God's redeeming work in society.

We live in a social system that has learned to accept divorce without condemnation, that expects very little from the home, and that has permitted the destruction of traditions without asking if there is anything to replace them.

Many who are studying the family and the home believe that in the next decade we will see a more distinct line of demarcation between secular and spiritual society. You probably will agree that the church and society need the family. Described by its Biblical model and precepts, the family unit has certain functions essential to the church. Understanding these Biblical teachings depends on the experiences within the family. For it is in the family that the child develops an awareness of God.

Whether we like it or not, it becomes the family's responsibility more than any other institution's to provide warmth, nurture, security, and the stimulation of verbalized ideas and widely selected experiences.

It is within the home and family that the child should share in reading aloud the holy Scriptures. The child can learn the communication of prayer and the consciousness of his relationship with the Heavenly Father. Devotions are vital even if difficult to establish.

When my children were growing up one of our first prayers was the Lord's Prayer. On one occasion I preached a series of sermons on the Lord's Prayer and as an introduction the entire congregation joined in quoting this prayer. My oldest daughter, then about 6 years old, was quite disturbed following the service. I inquired as to her concern and she said, "Everybody is using our prayer!" The Lord's Prayer had become something very special and personal to her and her sister. It is in the home that children develop this awareness of a personal relationship with God through prayer.

Those who minimize the importance of the home have not to this point been able to suggest a replaceable center of moral development for the child. For, in fact, there is no worthy substitute. The church can be a supplement but certainly not a replacement. The church must be careful not to weaken the family through programs that usurp family functions. Constant watch must be made to insure there is "also family time." Later chapters will speak to this issue.

Dr. Ward has suggested that great points of stress from the secular world are already visible, such as: materialism and competitive accumulation of things; pride and privilege based on status, class, power, and sex; pressures to conform; and blind acceptance of behaviorism in education and in management.

The issue of influences goes far beyond what TV programs our children should be allowed to watch and whether or not they should attend a "Christian school," for we are now in an era so challenging that all of our thoughts must be reevaluated in light of Biblical precepts. How do we view our families? Do we see them as part of God's redeemed society? Are we willing to separate ourselves from the greed and selfishness that characterizes much of our affluent society and see human needs as our responsibility?

The church must lift its prophetic voice in the pulpit and in the classroom and remind us of the nature of the family and its relationship to God's covenant. The Christian family will contrast more and more with the secular family because we have a "sense of history" and a "sense of commitment." We are indeed "in the world but not of the world" and this is becoming more and more a challenge. Let us examine in our families, "What would Jesus do and how would Jesus live?"

Let us recognize in our families (supplemented by our Sunday school and Christian education classes), the importance of instruction in morals, the need for consistency, the challenge of self-discipline on the part of each family member, and the sense of oneness God intended us to experience. There should, at the same time, be such love that we can grow to our potential and become creative within God's will for our lives.

The Generation Gap

One of the frightening aspects of the modern family is teenage rebellion. Rebellion shows itself in many forms. It may be excused by the term "generation gap," or it may be explained by sociologists or psychologists. Rebellion, however, can be very personal—between one teenager and one parent. The teenager may speak to his father or mother in the most degrading and disrespectful terms, or he may simply leave home without an explanation—thousands do it every year. This problem even touches Christian homes. How do we face it? How do we explain it?

Teenagers are at an in-between period. They are knowledgeable, yet they haven't completely developed their thinking or examined their responses. They are constantly rethinking their values. In early childhood most accept what they are taught but as they enter high school, and especially as they approach college age, they begin to question things. They meet people who have different values from those they have accepted. Television and their peers tell them there is another world. One by one their values are reconsidered. They may embark on a quest for reality, or they may express anger at some aspect of life. One university student said to me, "I have learned more than my parents, therefore I cannot accept what they have taught me."

Young people have often seen an emphasis on material values. They may be disillusioned by the "dead end" their parents have come to trying to achieve such ambitions. They may have discovered parental hypocrisy.

When a child reaches adolescence there is a personal up-heaval in every aspect of his life. Apart from sexual changes, tremendous fluctuations occur in his emotions which he may not know how to handle, and changes in family life or less parental control intensify these difficulties. The teenager can be happy one moment and depressed the next, ambitious today and despairing tomorrow.

One of the factors of teenage rebellion may be the home environment. If parents fail to cultivate a close relationship and do not provide an atmosphere in which their children feel free to discuss their problems, hopes, and fears, their children will feel insecure. When some young people ask their parents why they aren't permitted to do certain things, they receive this totally inadequate answer: "Because I said so." Parents are often guilty of concentrating on business success and failing to develop friendships with their children.

Some mothers have made their mark in society and even given themselves to church work, but spent little time with their children. It must be realized the answer to teenage rebel-lion lies with parents. They must take a second look at their own values. If they aren't sure of their values, they should ask their children—they will know. If parents are overly concerned with buying a second or third car, purchasing a vacation cot-tage, or taking an expensive trip, and have forgotten to cultivate honesty, sincerity, and reliability, their children will see it.

Both men and women should learn the value of touch, of expressing affection, of holding their children from earliest infancy on through the teenage years. Children will know if love is to be found in their home. Parents should provide a spiritual atmosphere and build their home on God's require-ments.

I remember the story one set of my daughter's grandparents told after she had spent a few days with them. We were meeting them halfway to bring her home. After we met, the question was asked, "Do you want to stay a few more days at PawPaw and Grandmommy's house?" Christi considered it, then said, "I had rather be with my own family."

If little children, as well as adolescents, have such a sense of security that they prefer being with their own family, then the rebellion problem will have been solved within the home.

Christian Family Life-style

I have already observed that a family is not a "Christian family" simply because each member confesses to being a born-again Christian. However, this is a beginning. We must remember, when we think about family histories, that we are right now writing our own family history and the kind of history we leave behind is our choice. God's plan for families cannot be divorced from theology; that is, the love of Christ for His church (Ephesians 5:25-27).

We who are of the Pentecostal persuasion and talk of the "Spirit-filled life" must recognize the Christian life-style should be applied to every sphere of living. We cannot be temperamentally unbalanced and still insist this is the Christian life-style. We must receive the Word of God and the will of God for us and then choose to walk in that knowledge of His Word and will. One of the great privileges of life is to know the ministry of the Holy Spirit in our individual lives, as well as in our family life. The Holy Spirit, with the fruit of the Spirit enumerated in Galatians 5:22, 23, can do much in the development of a Christian life-style.

Because we have come to know the forgiveness of sin and have received the blessed Holy Spirit of God, there ought to be a sense of joy and peace in our family life. This will affect our understanding of moral principles, our self-discipline, and our love for one another. The Christian family should offer opportunities to grow. It ought to be healthy in mind and body. The Christian home should be a place where one is alive spiritually with ideals and values that give life true meaning.

The best place for wholeness to take place is in a family; whether it is a single-parent family, a nuclear family, or the traditional extended family. The atmosphere of the home can contribute to wholeness. It is sad that the atmosphere of many homes contributes more to the breakdown of emotional and spiritual health than to wholeness.

What should the atmosphere of a Christian home be like? *First,* each member must be loved unconditionally. The time when a person has failed the most miserably is the very occasion he needs someone to believe in him and express confidence in him so he can rise above his failure. If "a significant other" can see beyond this momentary "failure" to the inner potential of the person's life, he will be affirmed in love. However, if he is judged by every individual act as though it were the totality of his being, then he will be doomed to a life of struggling for acceptance. You see, all of us grow best when someone offers support and encouragement during our time of need.

An obvious need, not only of children, but also of youth and adults, is self-esteem. To help the child grow in self-esteem, many times the parent must deliberately withhold judgment when the child fails to live up to expectations. All parents know that when the child comes home hurting, bruised, and battered, we must patch him up and send him on his way again.

And how often shall we be forgiving? Wasn't it Jesus who talked about 70 times 7? We must love our children, forgive them, encourage them, and send them out again with the conviction that they are "okay kids." I am not suggesting that we condone failure in our homes. What I am suggesting is the best way to avert failure. This does not mean we should neglect teaching values and principles; it means we must view the person as more important than the principle.

Second, it is important that we offer our children a "model." A positive mental attitude, like good religion, is more caught than taught.

A common denominator among successful persons is that at some point in their lives some significant person touched them and inspired them to achieve. It is tragic when a child is deprived of this experience. Hopefully, the significant person who inspires him will be a parent, but it could be a minister or Sunday school teacher. This need must be met by someone or the child will be robbed of his best chance for a fulfilled life. If we are going to be healthy, we need an example of what health is. So every father and every mother, every Sunday school teacher and every pastor must recognize the importance of being a model for positive Christian living.

Note Dorothy Law Nolte's insightful words:

Children Learn What They Live

If a child lives with criticism, He learns to condemn.
If a child lives with hostility, He learns to fight.
If a child lives with ridicule, He learns to be shy.
If a child lives with shame, He learns to feel guilty.
If a child lives with tolerance, He learns to be patient.
If a child lives with encouragement, He learns confidence.
If a child lives with praise, He learns to appreciate.
If a child lives with fairness, He learns justice.
If a child lives with security, He learns to have faith.
If a child lives with approval, He learns to like himself.
If a child lives with acceptance and friendship,
He learns to find love in the world.

A *third* necessity is providing challenges for healthy friction. Each of us is aware that man is a stress-seeking animal. The obvious question is: Are we living with good stress or bad stress in our families? We should remove the "distress" and keep the kind of stress that stimulates us to strive for excellency. People need something or someone to bounce off of. We need someone to whom we are accountable, otherwise we will lose the toughness necessary to cope with challenges.

Almost everyone who comes for counseling has the need to strengthen the "will." Some of the best help we can give is to create a climate in which the members of our family begin to take the responsibility for their own actions. The will becomes stronger as one faces obstacles and overcomes them. To overprotect those we care about is to strip from them the opportunity to develop wholeness in their life. So, if we want to help our family become whole and mature, let me suggest three things:

1. I will love each member of the family in the moments of their greatest failures.
2. I will try to model for them what it means to be a happy and productive human being.
3. I will allow them freedom to cope with life as it really is.

This will give opportunities to discover what life is about and to be creative, secure in a loving relationship. Then, as a family, we can discover God's will and purpose for our lives. Let us as parents be challenged as we look at family life today. Let us set some goals as to the kind of family we want and then work toward those goals.

C. S. Lewis, in *Mere Christianity* (New York: Macmillan Publishing Co., 1964), says: "God cannot give us happiness and peace apart from Himself, because it is not there. There is no such thing." So let us allow God the place of preeminence in our family's life-style.

The following "Christian Family Inventory" might suggest some ways to strengthen your family or encourage families in your Sunday school classes. Consider the inventory, then discuss with all family members what God is saying to you about the strengths and weaknesses in your family's life-style.

Inventory

Worship	Yes	No
1. We say grace at mealtime.	___	___
2. We conduct family devotions each day.	___	___
3. We attend Sunday morning worship service.	___	___
4. We attend Sunday evening worship service.	___	___
5. We are usually on time.	___	___
6. We bring our Bibles.	___	___
7. We give tithes and offerings regularly.		
	___	___

Study

1. We attend Sunday school regularly.   ___ ___
2. We prepare our lesson each week.   ___ ___
3. We attend the midweek activities of our church as a family.   ___ ___

Service

1. We invite others to attend our church.   ___ ___
2. We make phone and personal calls on visitors to our church.   ___ ___

3. We witness and invite others in other ways.

4. Our home has a Christian hospitality witness to all who visit.

Summary

There are many areas in our western culture that are threats to our Christian life-style. Jesus long ago said, "You are in the world but not of the world." We are part of our society, but we must be different from those who don't follow the Bible or our Lord. Let us choose to "build strong families."

Discussion Activities

1. All families experience stress at various times.
2. The influence of the media on our families.
3. The church exists "to minister" and one of its focuses must be on the family.
4. Leaders of the church define their concept of the "supporting role of the church" to our families.
5. The Christian family will more and more become a contrast to the secular family.

3

Husband/Wife Relationships

ALL OF US RECOGNIZE COMMUNICATION is a necessity of life. But often we fail to understand communication with our fellowman and sometimes we don't really communicate. Not only do we need to communicate with one another, we also need to communicate with God. This communication with God we call prayer and it ought to be two-way.

I shall never forget one couple I counseled. The husband explained all their problems. When he had finished his tirade, the wife said very quietly, "I think our big problem is communication." With that, he exploded, "Communication? I talk to you all the time. How could we have a problem of communication?"

Elements of Communication

The fact is, most of us have difficulties in communication. There are three parts to communication. The *first* is conveying the message, which is usually done by talking, although it may be nonverbal. The *second* is receiving the message, which is done primarily by listening. And the *third* is understanding the message. It is at this third point that the great breakdown in communication occurs.

The reason communication is so difficult in the husband/wife relationship is that the partners come from different emotional and psychological backgrounds, and perhaps even different geographic backgrounds. Whenever we attempt to communicate with one another, the message must be received through many filters. These filters are developed in our psychological makeup throughout our lives. They come from our parents, the school and church we attend, the area of the country in which we live, etc. Through these filters, we interpret the meaning of the message. That meaning may be accurate or inaccurate, depending on the effect of the filters. Therefore, it is very important that we check with one another to be sure we are hearing and understanding correctly what is being communicated to us verbally or nonverbally.

Communication in Marriage

It is a phenomenon observed in the role of pastoral counselor that couples who have no difficulty communicating before marriage develop this problem after marriage. How does this happen and why? Most would say the failure to communicate develops very gradually and for many reasons. Since this is not a book on communication, let me simply suggest that every couple needs time to be alone to communicate. It's wonderful to spend time with the children, but it's necessary for a couple to have time alone when they can openly express their feelings and their likes and dislikes and develop an understanding of each other.

Communication concerns both ideas and feelings. It involves openness, honesty, acceptance, and integrity. It requires talking things over. Most of us need to develop the art of being good listeners.

Here are some suggestions for better communication:

1. Don't take your spouse for granted. Don't suppose you already know how he feels or that he knows how you feel. Be verbal; express your feelings.

Perhaps you have heard the joke about the man who was asked by his wife, "Why don't you ever tell me you love me?"

His response was, "I told you the day I married you and if it ever changes, I will tell you."

There isn't much humor in that. Both the man and the woman need to hear words of appreciation and to understand the spouse's feelings.

2. Try to understand the other person's perspective. A great threat to communication is to believe you know what the other person is thinking. Give him a chance. When you understand the other person's viewpoint, it may surprise you how much sense it makes!

3. Try thinking before speaking. All of us have sensitive areas. If you are having a conflict, do not attack your mate's tender spots. Unkind words cannot be recalled; the hurt has already been done. So before you say something you may regret the rest of your life, stop and think.

4. Develop the habit of talking things over. All of us are busy and life is complicated, and we don't always take the time to try to understand one another. Plan time to be alone. Share common tasks together. The husband can join his wife in washing dishes or taking a walk, and money spent on a weekend away from home may be the best investment you've ever made. Take a mini-honeymoon occasionally.

5. Guard against using pressure tactics to get your own way. Sometimes we show our immaturity and selfishness by sarcasm, silence, or some other tactic. This just causes the other person to become defensive.

6. Do feel you have a right to express your feelings. If you disagree with your spouse, you have a right to say so. But help your partner to understand why you take the position you do and try to understand your partner's feelings.

7. Always be concerned about your partner. Become involved as much as possible in his everyday life. Try to understand where he is coming from, how he thinks and feels, and what his needs are.

8. Make major decisions after talking them over with each other. My wife and I long ago made an unwritten agreement that we wouldn't make a major decision without discussing it first. The husband and wife are inseparably bound together. I would recommend that no decision of any consequence be made without talking it over. The children should be included if the decision will affect them.

9. Be optimistic. Most problems have a solution, and a problem is half solved if you face it positively. If you do not approach it optimistically, your attitude itself may lead to failure.

10. Let your Christian faith be a source of strength. Pray about your problems and allow the fruit of the Spirit to develop in your life. This will sweeten communication, and the application of the golden rule will bring a peaceful atmosphere.

Intimacy

Parents and Christian educators need to emphasize the sanctity of the human body and the emotions, and stress that premarital relationships should be Christian and Biblical. In our promiscuous society "over familiarity" has become commonplace.

A necessary part of intimacy is developed from childhood. This is why we urge fathers and mothers to hold their children, touch them, and be accepting and loving, so the child may feel human closeness. A lack of a capacity for intimacy creates problems in some marriages.

An excellent book for Christian workers is *The Intimate Marriage,* by Howard and Charlotte Clinebell, Jr. (New York: Harper & Row Publishers, 1970). The Clinebells point out that many of the important questions asked by couples who come for marriage counseling have to do with the "search for relatedness in marriage," or intimacy.

Intimacy can be defined as closeness and unity. It presupposes such qualities as warmth, kindness, and love. Mankind has sought for these throughout the ages.

Intimacy becomes a challenge for teachers, for many children in our Sunday school do not acquire a sense of intimacy in their homes. If you find a child or young person who will not allow himself to become close to others, it may be he hasn't learned how to relate intimately to family members. He should be given attention to encourage him to be open and to share his feelings.

Teaching About Sex in the Home

One of the most encouraging developments of recent years is the Marriage Enrichment Movement. These seminars are valuable, but even if they aren't available, your marriage can become better. Developing a good marriage takes effort. In the past in the church, it has been difficult to broach the subject of sexuality, yet all of us are fully aware we are sexual beings. Somehow we have supposed that people would eventually relate to their sexuality.

However, in a world of great confusion and sometimes open rebellion against Biblical roles, it is encouraging to find materials available for help in marital and sexual enrichment. Two very fine books are Ed and Gaye Wheat's *Intended for Pleasure* (Old Tappan, NJ: Fleming H. Revell Co., 1977) and Tim and Beverly LaHaye's *The Act of Marriage* (Grand Rapids: Zondervan Publishing House, 1976). These books have been written from a Christian perspective and will be very helpful to anyone wanting to enrich their marital relationship.

I am convinced we adults have not been fulfilling our duties in teaching our children responsible sexuality. Many people are ashamed to discuss what God was not ashamed to create. There is a reason for this failure. Sometimes the parent feels awkward; revealing a personal inadequacy to deal with the subject. Much of the education most parents received was negative, and this is reflected by their uneasiness in discussing the subject.

Christian parents will realize that sexual issues involve religious values as well. Problems arise because of a lack of training in premarital or nonmarital situations. Many adult Christians would find it difficult to describe in detail the meaning of the adult sexual life. However, there's good news—as evidenced by the number of best-sellers dealing with sexuality—adults are searching. This holds hope for a positive attitude in the education of our children. A book I recommend on this subject is *Sexual Happiness in Marriage*, by Herbert J. Miles (Grand Rapids: Zondervan Publishing House, 1967). One chapter gives "A Christian Interpretation of Sex in Marriage," which is worth the price of the book.

Conflict Resolution

Earlier, we dealt with some of the methods to be used in general communication that are vital to conflict resolution. Because conflict resolution is often not understood and seldom practiced in marital life, and because I would like to encourage couples to face conflicts more openly, I want to deal with some basic steps of conflict resolution.

Some people think that because both marriage partners are Christians, they will never have conflicts. However, those who are married understand that conflicts do exist and it is important to resolve them in a Christian manner. In fact, it is normal for couples to have problems. The experience of most of us is that some problems surface in the day-by-day changes in our lives. Often people I counsel say, "My partner is not the same person I married." Certainly not, for marriage and human life are not static. Adjusting is a lifelong task, but it can be done—as many Christian couples are proving.

Marriage is the most intimate of all human relationships. Therefore, it holds the greatest potential for conflict. Conflict is not necessarily wrong or harmful, but the manner in which it is resolved determines whether it is damaging or not. Couples who learn conflict resolution can utilize conflicts to improve their communication and grow in intimacy.

Intimacy can grow when conflicts are faced openly and honestly and are resolved in the painful but rewarding process of growing understanding. Sometimes this calls for compromises. Basic to conflict resolution are a commitment to Christ and a commitment to one another in a lifelong relationship.

Both partners must learn to listen to the other's complaints and accept his feelings, even if the feelings are directed toward him. We must approach conflict resolution with the realization that enduring love is more than a feeling or tender emotion; it is also actions. Persons must not only feel they must also act in love. When conflicts arise, there must be a strong desire to resolve the differences and work at a no-fault, no-blame attitude. When a spouse takes the position that one must win and the other must lose, both partners will lose.

Suggestions for Conflict Resolution

1. Your first responsibility as a Christian is to pray. It may be possible to resolve the conflict between you and the Lord without ever taking it to your partner. Sometimes when you confess your faults to the Lord, you may see the problem is not worth the effort.

2. Keep to the here and now. Do not use yesterday's problems as ammunition for today's discussion. If you recall the past and use such words as "you always" or "you never," you will make the problem greater and you will show you haven't forgiven those past conflicts.

3. Keep to the one issue that is at the heart of the conflict.

4. Use "I" messages, such as "I am free." Express your feelings with "I" rather than "you." If you express your hurts by saying, "I feel very angry when . . . ," it will call for assistance to your need rather than threatening the other person.

5. Do not counterattack. If your spouse presents a complaint, do not respond, "You're just as bad!" There may be a legitimate reason for bringing the complaint.

6. Avoid mind reading. Do not attempt to analyze your partner's attitudes or motives. It is the heart of the conflict, the behavior itself, that must be dealt with.

7. Deal with the conflict as quickly as possible. Do not put off confrontation. Feelings must be dealt with and expressed in some manner.

8. Keep the emotions appropriate. Be sure the size of the emotions is appropriate for the size of the conflict.

9. Don't try to win in the conflict. It is important to remember that when one partner wins, the other must be a loser, and when one loses both of you lose. The goal should be to find a satisfactory solution so that both partners will come out as winners. For, in the Christian marriage, the two have become "one in Christ."

Suppose one partner feels a need or has a complaint. He talks to the Lord about it, but it still isn't resolved. What should he do? He can begin by announcing his intention to his mate: "I have a problem I need to talk over with you." He should state the complaint, and his spouse should listen without response. He should explain what is wrong and how he feels about it.

It is critical at this point that the person receiving the complaint does not defend himself, but listens and tries to understand by responding with such comments as, "I understand you to be saying. . . ." When the issue has been made clear and the feelings are understood, the next step can be taken—a proposed resolution to the conflict.

The person with the complaint should state clearly what is wanted. He should explain what it would mean to have it resolved and how it can benefit both partners. The partner receiving the complaint should respond to the suggested resolution and explain how he feels about the issue and the proposal for change. There are three options: the partner may agree with the request, he may disagree completely, or he may suggest a compromise. Depending on the size of the conflict, it may be necessary to allow some time to ponder the situation before further discussion. In the meantime, the emotions will have a chance to settle and God may provide creative alternatives.

Next, the couple must ask for and grant forgiveness. There is no room for unresolved feelings of anger or resentment between the husband and the wife. Forgiveness should be received and asked by each. This does not imply that you have agreed with the partner's position.

Because we are considering the Christian and Biblical marriage, it would be worthwhile to look at God's kind of love as portrayed in 1 Corinthians 13:

> Slow to suspect—Quick to trust
> Slow to condemn—Quick to justify
> Slow to offend—Quick to depend
> Slow to expose—Quick to shield
> Slow to reprimand—Quick to forbear
> Slow to belittle—Quick to appreciate
> Slow to demand—Quick to give
> Slow to provoke—Quick to conciliate
> Slow to hinder—Quick to help
> Slow to resent—Quick to forgive

These qualities will work wonders in a marriage relationship. Try them and see the wisdom of God!

I have studied and restudied the New Testament passages relating to the family. In Ephesians 6, Paul speaks to both children and parents when he says: "Children, obey your parents in the Lord: for this is right. Honor thy father and mother" (vv. 1, 2). But then he says to fathers: "And, ye fathers, provoke not your children to wrath: but bring them up in the nurture and admonition of the Lord" (v. 4).

As Paul speaks to fathers, he deals first with the negative, the provoking "not." Fathers should not stir their children up by harsh rules or unreasonable expectations; they should "bring them up in the nurture and admonition of the Lord." The responses of young people in our society may be crying out to us of the need to balance relationships between parents and children. Parents should set positive examples and not be guilty of driving their children to rebellion.

Discussion Activities

1. We use message filters in the art of communication.
2. Why couples communicate before marriage but have problems after the honeymoon.
3. Communication involves feelings and ideas.
4. Conflict is normal; some stress is necessary, but it must be resolved without a "loser."
5. God's kind of love (1 Corinthians 13) can revolutionize a family.

4

Family Relationships

THANK GOD FOR THE MANY BOOKS available on the family and home. Even some of the titles speak volumes of truth, like Knofel Staton's *Home Can Be a Happy Place* (Cincinnati, OH: Standard Publishing)—I want to shout, "Sure it can!" Then there's Wayne E. Rickerson's *Getting Your Family Together* (Glendale, CA: Gospel Light/Regal Books, 1977)—I want to urge all parents and children, "Yeah! Let's do it!" And there's Howard Hendrick's *Heaven Help the Home* (Wheaton, IL: Victor Books, 1974)—I pray, "God, please do!"

Relationships within the family are always challenging. If we would all develop a relationship of love and trust with the God who made us, it would be much easier to relate to His children. Dr. Richard Dobbins observed that one of the problems with Americans is too many of our relationships are with "things." We relate to machines—like automobiles and televisions. Too few of our relationships are with the "people" we love.

Shared experiences are important. Dr. Dobbins points out, in *Train up a Child* (Grand Rapids: Baker Book House), that many times our worship is not a shared experience. Ideally, it should be parents and children who love each other, all sharing a time with God.

In our concern for proper parenting and successful teaching, we must focus on the child and "significant others," us adults.

Child/Parent Relationships

John M. Drescher, in his book *Seven Things Children Need* (Scottdale, PA: Herald Press, 1976), tells of a boy handing his dad his report card. While his father stands silently, in a state of shock, the boy asks, "Dad, do you think those grades are the result of heredity or environment?"

Many parents today are not sure whether their children's problems are the result of what they inherited or learned from their parents, or are caused by the pressures and patterns of our society. Child rearing has never been an easy assignment and it seems harder today than ever before. Children should be recognized as a sacred trust from God to the family, whether they are natural born or adopted (Psalm 127:3). Because children are our responsibility, both those in our home and those in our church, we must seek to do our best in making them what God has given them the potential to become.

For many years, and perhaps throughout history, the role of the mother as the person who brings new life into the world has been stressed. "The hand that rocks the cradle rules the world." I would not minimize for a moment the significant role of mothers. No child, or adult, can help but be affected psychologically and emotionally if the mother has not fulfilled her role. But because of the lack of understanding of the father's role, we will focus on it.

The Role of the Father

Dr. Kenneth Chafin, in his book *Is There a Family in the House?* (Waco, TX: Word Books, 1978), tells of responses children gave to a survey used in his church. To the questions, "What are mothers like?" and "What are fathers like?" about half the children spoke of functions that are performed or relationships that exist. For example: "Fathers and mothers are people who live together"; "Parents take care of you"; "A mother washes dishes, cleans house, and has babies"; "A father works at the office, makes money, and fixes things that break." While the other half of the children responded in terms of feelings: "Parents take care of you, love each other, play with you, guide you, etc."

Dr. Chafin noted:

While mothers become the primary parent, the older the child, the more impact the father has. Perhaps the impact is because father isn't home all the time and this points out the need for quality time when the father is home.

I have noticed in counseling with young adults, when I ask the question, "Which parent do you admire the most?" almost without exception the men respond, "I admire my mother the most," while the women respond, "I admire my father the most." I'm not sure the reason for this or even if it is consistent with the findings of others. Perhaps the daughter is looking for a model for a male/husband/father and the son is looking for a model for a female/wife/mother. The fact is, we owe it to our children to use our influence for good as they develop their sense of masculinity and femininity.

Many men think it is not masculine to hug their children, to touch them, or to verbally express their love. However, the Bible indicates the father is under the authority of God—and God is love—and he has the role of providing the children with expressions of love. Do not be ashamed or afraid to hold your son or daughter. If there is a good relationship in early childhood, when they are teenagers you probably will find they will still appreciate that expression of love found in a hug.

The father has the spiritual role of priest of his house. It is significant that Jesus said: "Where two or three are gathered together in my name, there am I in the midst of them." Mother, father, and child become the nucleus of the body of Christ. Let the father assume his role of spiritual leadership.

I think it is important for the Sunday school to try to place men in the early age-levels of the Sunday school, so boys and girls will not identify it as just a woman's place. Husband-and-wife teaching teams work well in many Sunday schools.

A father is responsible for the training of his children for both secular and spiritual pursuits (Proverbs 22:6). He must never lose sight of the importance of his Christian example to his mate and his children. This involves his personal devotional life and his leadership in his home, church, and community.

The Role of the Mother

The mother's role is a demanding role. She supports the authority of her husband and sets an example of what a Christian woman is like. (Study Titus 2:3-5; 1 Peter 3:1-4; and Ephesians 5:22-24, 33.) As a homemaker, the mother is responsible for the orderliness and organization of the home. She has the major input into the education and learning experiences of her children. The quality of mothering a child receives during his preschool years is tremendously important for the development of his personality and self-image.

Many women in our society work outside the home either because they are career-oriented or because of necessity. If it is necessary for the mother to work, she must guard against bringing home dissatisfactions which would irritate family relationships. Because of her assignment as a mother, she must try to balance her career and her homemaking roles. All family responsibilities should be considered with the children in mind.

The Role of the Child

The child's role is not always clearly defined in the minds of parents. Children are gifts from God, and with them comes the responsibility "to rear and nurture" them. However, this relationship is not permanent. Our responsibility must always be with the view of maturing the child, until we have worked ourselves out of a job. When the child becomes an adult in chronological years, hopefully he is also an adult in emotional development. The family is the context within which a child develops a strong selfhood and becomes a person who is warm and accepting in personality and has conquered selfishness in the growing-up process.

In a society that puts tremendous pressure on children, it is easy for parents to become either overpossessive or overpermissive. Either extreme causes insecurity in the child. When a parent is too possessive, the child's personality becomes warped. It is hard to face this fact, but an overpossessive parent loves the child primarily for what the child does for the parent. This is selfish love and it hurts both the parent and the child. The other extreme, the overpermissive parent, furnishes no clear guidelines or framework within which a child should live, so the child feels insecure.

I shall never forget one teenager I counseled who said, "I wish my parents would give me rules so I would know that somebody cared." Although I personally believe the rules should be few, they should consistently build stability and security.

The Role of Grandparents

The role of grandparents is something we have known but failed to utilize. In our mobile society, grandparents often do not live near their grandchildren. This is a loss to both the grandparents and the grandchildren. Whenever it is possible, grandparents can make a great contribution to their grandchildren's well-being by supplying them with love and at the same time transmitting values. The grandchildren will also provide the grandparents with a sense of fulfillment. If the grandparents are Christians, they can instill in their grandchildren a love for God, prayer, the Bible, and the church.

Lois Duncan focuses on one aspect of grandparents in "Grandfather Days":

Grandfather days have a special glow,
They move at a pace that is sure and slow
With a different rhythm, a different rhyme,
A blend of today and another time
When life was simple and dreams were clear.
A grandfather speaks, and a child can hear
The quiet music behind his words–
The winds of spring, or the cry of birds
In an autumn sky, or the sound of rain
Making puddles grow in a country lane.
As years slip by to a further day,
A grandfather's love comes a long, long way.
When pressures grow, as they sometimes will,
I close my eyes, and I find it still—
The peace—the sweetness—the golden haze—
The gentle magic of grandfather days.

Much work needs to be done in the church in utilizing senior citizens. They may become "adopted grandparents" and establish relationships that will overcome the lack of an extended family. Christian educators should give this consideration in the functioning and structure of the church.

The style of homelife should reflect the Christian's witness. Although the line of authority and discipline is clearly delineated in Scripture, parents choose whether their family will have a "closed life-style" (dictatorial; rules and decisions come from above and are carried out by other members) or an open one in which all family members are free to share and communicate.

I counseled one family, consisting of a husband, wife, son, and daughter, in which the husband did all the talking. He told me communication was no problem in their family. I smiled at the wife and expected a response, but she said nothing. After a couple of sessions, she began to share some of her feelings and they were very contrary to those of her husband. The children still did not open up and express their feelings.

The family began what they called a "family council" meeting every Saturday morning following breakfast. After a few weeks, the children started to reveal their feelings. A closeness developed among them all. And for the first time, the father understood the wall he had built between him and his family. After several months, the teenage son and daughter felt free to express a viewpoint that differed from their father's, and they learned to compromise and to understand their parents' point of view. They also developed an appreciation for the rules agreed on in their family. Discipline was simplified once there was some input from all family members. Children sometimes have difficulty when life-styles are in conflict.

Sunday school teachers should try to understand why one child is silent in class while the others are very verbal. It may be a reflection of the life-style at home. The teacher should try to draw out and encourage the child to participate.

The Things Children Need

I mentioned John M. Drescher's book earlier, and from it I have drawn the following ideas on the needs of children.

First, children need a sense of significance or *personal worth*. If we feel we are of no value and we do not like ourselves, how can we believe anyone else will like us? There are a great many people seeking help from pastors and other counselors who are plagued with inferiority feelings stemming from their childhood. It is the young person who has not gained a proper sense of significance that races his car and "burns rubber" on the highway, draws attention by his brash speech or dress, or becomes obnoxious to the rest of society by other overt behavior. As adults, these individuals continue to call attention to themselves, desiring to be recognized as persons, by striving for honors, deserved or undeserved.

No father or mother should ever be guilty of belittling a child. A parent can either give or rob a child of self-respect. Ridicule, sarcasm, and contempt directed at a child, produce feelings of inferiority in him and must be avoided. To laugh at a child is inexcusable.

How does a parent build a sense of significance in the child? A parent's attitude toward himself is important. If the parent has a sense of worth, he can convey this to his child. A Sunday school teacher can build self-esteem in a child by giving recognition based not on what he does but on who he is as a person. Parents should let their children help around the house even though their work isn't up to an adult's level of competence; Sunday school teachers can do the same thing.

A person's name is very important. This is true of children also. Parents should introduce their friends to their children, and Sunday school teachers should know and call their pupils by name. When a child is spoken to, he should be allowed to answer for himself. Parents who do not respect their children as persons want to assert their own importance by answering for them.

Children should have the privilege of making choices and, whenever possible, their choices should be respected. A child interprets the time you spend with him as saying, "You are important to me." When a Sunday school teacher spends time outside the class with his pupils, he says to them, "You are important." Those who work with children and have studied the problems of our society agree that helping a person to like himself is one of the greatest gifts one can give.

Second, a child needs *security*. This is an innate craving. We've all used the expression "security blanket." This simply means that when the child has that blanket he feels secure.

Sometimes parents and educators do certain things that create insecurity. For example, when there is tension and quarreling between parents, the child feels caught in the middle. A family that moves to a new community can be sure that feelings of insecurity will arise in the child. Lack of discipline creates insecurity. Constant criticism and insecurity within the parents also cause problems in the children.

Christian educators must remember they are dealing with persons, not lessons. They must provide security within the classroom and be dependable so the children will know what to expect. Discipline should build security in the children.

Parents who sincerely love one another and express this love openly help the child feel secure. And love for the child, expressed by the parents, also builds security. Stability may be seen in family unity and experienced in doing things together. Proper discipline is important. A child needs to know what is expected of him, and discipline administered fairly and in love brings peace and not turmoil to the child. Earlier, I mentioned the importance of touching the child. Parents should be aware of how vital it is that they hold and touch the child; this will give him a sense of belonging.

A third need is *acceptance.* Some children are accepted when they succeed but not when they fail. Why do children feel they are not accepted? Children who are criticized develop feelings of failure, rejection, and inadequacy. No child should ever be compared with others, for this conveys inferiority and a lack of acceptance. Seeking to force a child to achieve the unfulfilled dreams of the parent causes him to feel unaccepted. Imposing expectations on a child in an unrealistic manner is cruel. A child of whom too much is expected feels rejected for what he is. Acceptance means the child is liked at all times regardless of his acts or ideas.

How does one build acceptance? By recognizing the child as a unique person. Every child should know his parents like him just as he is. The child needs to find satisfaction in his achievements. He must receive verbal and nonverbal expressions of love; that he is wanted and really enjoyed. Accepting the child's friends builds acceptance. Learning to listen to what the child is saying conveys acceptance, as does treating him as a person of worth and allowing him to develop in his own way.

Fourth, every child needs *to be loved.* The real question is: Do our children know they are loved? We *learn* to love. A child does not know how to love when he is born. As he receives love, he learns to respond to it and give love in return. Parents who love each other enhance the child's ability to love. Love is visible acts, thoughtfulness, and kindness. Communication of love is essential; love must be spoken.

Love calls for action. A father may say, "I love you, son," but if he never has any time for the boy, the message is clear. Love requires us to be willing to listen. Most parents find it hard to listen at times. Everyone is busy and has responsibilities, but listening carefully to the expressed needs of a child communicates, "I love you."

The fifth need of a child is *praise.* Failing to praise their children is a common fault of parents. I have sometimes given an assignment to parents to keep a record of how many times they praise their children. Quite often they discover they criticize many times more than they praise. A way to change this would be for the parent to require himself to praise his child everyday.

Everybody needs praise. Why not have a compliment or a word of praise for everyone you touch as you go through life? Sunday school teachers can build confidence in children with a word of praise. They should go light on criticism but heavy on praise. The child's performance can be praised. He should be praised for what he is responsible for, rather than what he is not.

The child who has the approval of others will not need to be proud or boastful. Praise is especially needed from the people who are important to the child. They are the "significant others." Parents ought to be the most significant persons to their child. Sunday school teachers can also fill this need. Praise must be sincere. Keep in mind that the sooner praise comes, the better. When an achievement is made, give the encouraging word and praise at that moment. If a child lives with praise, he learns to appreciate. A child needs praise every day to develop proper attitudes.

I heard Dr. Howard Hendricks say: "If I had my life to live over, and my family to begin again, I would praise my children more." I think that's important for all of us to remember.

Sixth, children need *discipline.* Perhaps an entire chapter needs to be given to the matter of discipline. The secret of discipline in our homes, lies in establishing the order of relationships as set forth in the Word of God. It would be worthwhile to read again Ephesians 5:21, 24; 6:1. The commandment to honor and obey parents requires that children see the kind of discipline in their parents that merits honor and engenders obedience.

Discipline involves the total molding of the child's character through encouraging good behavior and correcting unacceptable behavior. To be sure, punishment is a part of discipline and a temporary deterrent, but punishing bad behavior does not automatically produce good behavior. The purposes of discipline must be clearly defined.

Some Ground Rules for Balancing Discipline

1. Rules should be reasonable. This can be established by discussion with those involved. Both parents should agree on the rules.
2. Rules need to be communicated in the language of the child. Be sure they understand the rules.
3. Rules should be consistently enforced. To threaten or nag is only to lead a child into insecurity. The actual methods of control are never as important as the parent's consistency and an ever-present spirit of wanting to help the child.

Dr. James Dobson's *Dare to Discipline* (Wheaton, IL: Tyndale House Publishers, 1970) is a very practical book. He gives five keys to discipline.

The *first* principle is to develop respect for the parent. The parent/child relationship provides the basis for all future relationships for the child. Parents must earn the right to control their child in the eyes of the child.

The *second* suggestion is to recognize that communication often improves after punishment. The emotional ventilating following punishment relieves the tension, and a child may want to express love by hugging his parents. The parents should respond with open arms and not reject the child.

Control without nagging is the *third* principle. It is all too easy to continue telling a child the same thing. The child then develops the idea that you have to speak several times before it means anything.

The *fourth* principle is not to saturate the child with excessive materialism. Temporary deprivation will increase appreciation in a child, but excessive giving of things diminishes the thrill of receiving.

The *fifth* suggestion is to avoid extremes in control and love. A parent who is harsh causes a child to live in constant fear and he becomes unable to make his own decisions. The child is totally dominated and humiliated. Permissiveness is equally tragic because the child is taught that he can get what he wants by going after it, and he loses respect for others.

Children obey and honor their parents, primarily, because the parents do their best and the children respond to love, understanding, and meaningful relationships. Fortunately, a person doesn't have to be perfect to be a parent. Parents should recognize individual differences in their children; no two children can be dealt with the same way.

The seventh need of a child is *God.* Harmful views of life are learned by statements like: "God does not love you when you are bad," or, "If you will be a good girl, you will go to heaven." The Bible teaches important principles about God. Parents should be right with God themselves. Those who only tell their children religious facts are not fulfilling their responsibilities. Children can understand God, love, and forgiveness only to the extent that they experience them in the relationships of the family and home. The Bible puts the responsibility of the religious training of children squarely on the parents. Read again Psalm 78:1-8 and 2 Timothy 3:14-16. The Bible tells us parents' instruction should be constant and continuous.

Spiritual Lessons

We must understand how our responsibilities, from a Biblical perspective, relate to the child's present and eternal well-being. Basic to this is salvation through Jesus Christ. Parents sometimes are hesitant to speak to their children about spiritual matters, but it is of great importance that the child hears from his parents their concern for his salvation. Pray with the child; listen to his concerns. At the earliest opportunity, lead your child to a personal faith in Jesus Christ. Teachers may reinforce this effort or do what isn't done by parents by using the Sunday school to communicate the love of God and lead to a personal commitment to Jesus Christ.

It is in the home a child should first learn obedience. Many parents fail to receive proper respect because they do not live respectful lives before their children. Parents who do not display Christianity before their children oftentimes fail to receive the honor the Bible speaks of. Parents who want their children to be peaceable and in command of their own behavior must show how this is done by the way they live their lives. Self-discipline can be taught, and it is usually learned in three stages.

The first step is *conformity* to family expectations. When a child learns what is expected of him and then receives positive encouragement in meeting those expectations, he begins to learn self-discipline. *Identification* occurs when the child admires his parents and decides he wants to be like them. He soon becomes like the parents without actually trying. And, finally, *internalization* occurs. This is the process by which the learned values are made personal. Behavior becomes spontaneous because it is now part of the child's personality.

The importance of positive words cannot be overstated. It is a challenge for parents and Christian educators to speak positively of the child, of the church, and of the people of God. Negative words build insecurity, hostility, and failure into the thinking of the child. Do not allow yourself to give in to anger and make a disparaging remark about the child or others. The hurt and damage that result can never be totally eradicated. Let us pray often the prayer found in Psalm 19:14: "Let the words of my mouth, and the meditations of my heart, be acceptable in thy sight, Oh Lord, my strength, and my redeemer."

Discussion Activities

1. Fathers under God's authority should provide their children with expressions of love.

2. All family responsibilities must be considered with the children in mind.

3. Children are a gift from God.

4. To laugh at a child is inexcusable.

5. Rules for a child should be reasonable, communicated in understandable language, and consistently enforced.

REASONS Why Children Get Exasperated

1- UNANNOUNCEd RUlES

2- RulES That Change

3- OVErPUNishEd oNE dAy ANd uNderpuNished the NEXt dAy

4- PuNish the child to FAST

5

Family
Stewardship

WHEN ANY PERSON BECOMES A PARENT he inherits many responsibilities, and the greatest is management of the best gift of all—life. Not only do parents have to account for their own lives they also have to bear responsibility for their children's lives as well. What a tremendous responsibility and privilege!

Everyone is born a steward. And our Creator has an unconditional claim on all we are and all we have. We must follow His will to be successful.

The first commandment for stewardship came when God instructed Adam and Eve in the Garden of Eden to exercise dominion. Also, He instructed them to "be fruitful and multiply, and fill the earth, and subdue it." (See Genesis 1:26-31, *NASB*.)

To assist man and woman in fulfilling this responsibility of stewardship, God instituted the family with express purposes including: bearing the image of God; procreating other humans; modeling God's laws; replenishing the earth; fellowshipping with God and each other; and providing mutual support and nurture.

Stewardship in Scripture

Contrary to popular belief, a study of the Biblical concept of stewardship reveals the term encompasses more than just managing money wisely. A steward was usually a personal slave (Genesis 39:4) who was entrusted with all his master's business dealings; and, although he received many concessions, everything he owned belonged to his master. He constantly tried to bring honor to his master's name. Periodically he was called by his master to give account of his business dealings.

In the New Testament the apostles frequently called themselves servants or slaves (Romans 1:1; Philippians 1:1; 2 Peter 1:1; Jude 1), recognizing that all they had belonged to their Lord.

Jesus described two kinds of stewards in Matthew 24 and 25 as the wise and wicked stewards respectively.

So, the scriptural meaning of stewardship is *management* of that which has been entrusted for safekeeping. A steward is only an administrator, not the owner, for he simply holds things in trust for another.

In broad terms, then, true stewardship includes: time, attitudes, prayer, material possessions, service, education, nature, career, friends, abilities, hospitality, leisure, influence, testimony, and so on. Both tangibles and intangibles are involved.

Stewardship of Treasure

Our culture teaches us to measure success by the extent of one's material wealth. We are encouraged to love things and use people when, instead, we should love *people* and use things.

Often in a couple's quest for worldly possessions, they blindly fall into traps from which it is very difficult to escape. And, their family is ensnared along with them! Jesus pointedly warned: "Where your [family's] treasure is, there will your [family's] heart be also" (Matthew 6:21). It is not wrong to acquire possessions so long as you don't sell out to a spirit of greed in pursuing them. And men are particularly prone to fail in this regard since they find to a great extent their personal identity through industry and work.

The real issue in the stewardship of treasure is not one of supplying vital necessities for our families, but rather an issue of proper Christian values. Where do most parents place their values and priorities when it comes to wants and needs?

Even adults play the childhood game of "I want it." There is a hard-to-control urge in all of us to acquire more than basic needs. No one is going to balance your wants-needs list but yourself.

We are living in an era of staggering financial debt. Never before in the history of the world have so many owed so much to so few. And the debts keep rising. Today Americans hold over 600 million credit cards to maintain their unprecedented lifestyles. Christian parents have a moral obligation to face the implications of unwise credit buying.

Parents need to concentrate on following sound management principles for themselves and their children. They should avoid accumulating debts and limit their dealings to cash purchases as much as possible by:

—Tithing and saving
—Cautious shopping
—Studying the legal entanglements of credit
—Appraising the total market before buying
—Wisely using credit cards
—Avoiding impulse buying
—Planned spending
—Preparing a family budget
—Teaching children stewardship values

Regular tithing is one of the Christian family's greatest privileges. God challenges us to try Him and see if He will not honor His word and pour out a manifold blessing (Malachi 3:8-10). Practical teaching on stewardship and modeling generosity in the home will please the heart of God, strengthen the church, and entitle the children to future blessings.

Proper family stewardship will require a percentage of the family income going for investments and savings. One of the few hedges against rising inflation is wise investments. A recent poll of 165 leading members of the Securities Industry Association suggests sound investments, in order: common stocks, money market funds, municipal bonds, short-term treasuries, corporate bonds, and real estate (*U.S. News and World Report*, December '79, p. 84).

Responsible stewards will want to shelter their family's future through adequate *health, life, auto,* and *home* insurance protection and proper health care. A mortgage insurance policy (usually term life insurance) on the home will be especially comforting to the entire family.

Christian concern requires us to go the second mile to appraise ourselves of national, state, and local laws of estate planning. An up-to-date will is a necessity if a family is to avoid high taxes and staggering probate costs.

Every family should prepare an annual budget to teach Christian stewardship and guarantee balance between expenditures and income. Provision should be made in the budget for investments, housing, services, food, and other operating expenses. Parents need to inform their children of family budgeting practices and teach them how to begin managing their own monies on a graduated basis. The first of each new year is an excellent time to deal with these matters.

George M. Bowman, in his outstanding best-seller *How to Succeed With Your Money* (Chicago: Moody Press, 1974), relates a good financial formula must include: a plan to save; a way to control all living costs; and a solution to the problem of debt. He suggests "the 10-70-20 plan." After you have paid your taxes and your obligations to God, set aside 10 percent of your income for savings and investments. Next, live on seven-tenths (70 percent) of your net income. Then, never pay more than 20 percent to retire debts.

Christian family stewardship involves not only tangible but also intangible assets. Our Christian stewardship demands a testimony of fiscal responsibility and balanced budgeting.

Stewardship of Time

When I ask family-enrichment seminar participants to list the major ways families use time when at home, invariably they will recount: eating, sleeping, working, arguing, playing, reading, watching television, praying, caring for children, talking, and so on.

Then when asked to pick the top three time-consumers for the average family, television viewing is always in the group.

Since children spend approximately 1 percent of their time at church, 16 percent of their time at school, and 83 percent of their time at home, parents must put a high priority on meaningful "together time" in the home. Each day both parents and children make decisions, which, in time, form into permanent patterns (life-styles) of home behavior.

It would be good to analyze your family's time usage, which should include, in addition to the statements above:nurturing, enrichment, relationship building, worship, communication, and mutual support. Basically, time should be balanced among God, family, others, and yourself.

I am concerned, along with parents and professionals, about the subtlety and emotional force of contemporary television commercials and programming. Dr. Rose K. Goldsen says television is more than just a little fun and entertainment: "It's a whole environment, and what it does bears an unpleasant resemblance to behavior modification on a mass scale." We are not only rushing out to buy the products advertised, we are also being sold a life-style that is hostile to our Christian beliefs and basic family values.

Television commercials have become the most powerful selling medium in America. Enormous power resides in this mass symbol-making process. Each day 730,000 commercials are broadcast to the American people. The average child watches 5 hours of television advertising a week. By high school graduation, he will have seen more than 350,000 commercials.

One of the catchy phrases the advertisers use is: "We do it all for you. . . ." The fact is, the average family of four pays over $100 a year for "free" television! And we help support this $6-billion-a-year advertising industry by spending 3 to 10 times more for a heavily advertised brand name than for an identical less well-known brand.

Families and Christian teachers can promote television awareness among their children and students by doing some of the following activities:

1. Watch several T.V. commercials as a family project. Help children understand gimmicks, techniques, and "emotional hooks" that link the products with good feelings.

2. Show that the advertisers appeal to the basic fears of inadequacy and fantasies of wish fulfillment in four essential areas: family, intimacy, vitality, and success.

3. Young children often believe all commercials are "true." Ask your child(ren) to talk about specific commercials to see what he or she is understanding—or misunderstanding.

4. Keep a family T.V. log for 2 weeks—to find out who is watching T.V., what they are watching, and how much time is spent in front of the tube. (Presently, the average estimate for small children is up to approximately 40 hours a week.)

5. Follow the above activity with a discussion on how to limit viewing and concentrate on creative individual and family pursuits.

Suggested Resources

1. Research findings, a quarterly newsletter, legislative reports, and other resources are available from Action for Children's Television, 46 Austin Street, Newtonville, MS 02160.

2. *T.V.—The Anonymous Teacher* is a 15-minute color film about the effects of television on children; available from Mass Media Ministries, 2116 N. Charles Street, Baltimore, MD 21218, phone 301-727-3270.

Every member of the family needs a regular retreat from an often hostile world where they can replenish their innate strengths, find comfort and support, and be transformed into the image of Christ. Parents are responsible to provide just such an enriching, nurturing environment in the home.

How often we neglect a chief element of Christian stewardship by allowing debilitating influences to siphon off the creativity and unique potentials of our family and home.

Christian leaders need to rally to the beleaguered parents with guidance and practical training. Hopefully, every home can, in time, become more than just a home full of Christians—a truly Christian home with abundant nurture for each family member and a preserving influence on the community for the kingdom of God.

Stewardship of Abilities

Parents and Christian leaders have an equal responsibility as guardians of their own and their children's creative abilities.

There are individual qualities of natural and spiritual endowment which must be recognized, cultured, and given opportunity of expression.

The Christian home should be characterized as a developmental center to lead children to recognize their own unique abilities. The parents' life must first reflect proper utilization of their own abilities as a basic foundation to guiding children to their greatest potential.

It would be a worthwhile venture for parents to help their children discover their natural abilities by exposing them to family roots. I will long remember conversations with my elderly uncle concerning our family's interesting European ancestry. After my forefathers came to the new world, they carried out the family traditions through furniture- and wheel-making. Even though I'm not a carpenter, I feel that vital information has helped me recognize innate tendencies and certain abilities.

An Old Testament example that assures me of the communication of values and abilities from one generation to another is the occasion when Isaac redug the wells of Abraham his father (Genesis 26:18). He had no doubt observed, as a child, his dad digging wells to supply the family's needs.

Even though most behavior is learned, it is unwise for parents to forcefully mold children into life-styles that are unrealistic for them. Great heartache and deep-seated rebellion are usually generated when parents indiscriminately impose their will on their child.

On the contrary, parents should cultivate each child's abilities at the child's own rate of development. And, at the same time, they should help the child understand his personal responsibility to realize his maximum potential under God. Our children will accelerate their overall growth if we:

1. Lead them to practice regular personal devotions and Bible-reading habits.

2. Steer them into productive use of their work and leisure time. Productiveness is a basic rule of Scripture. Excess television viewing is detrimental to their development.

3. Teach them the innate and acquired skills parents have and guide them in practicing similar skills.

4. Show them how to recognize God's will for their lives in Scripture, circumstances, and through prayer.

5. Explore every possibility with them of options for different vocations and avocations.

6. Cultivate those abilities that become evident during their development.

7. Evaluate their feelings about their abilities.

8. Look for and affirm evidences of success and productivity.

9. Monitor confirmation of their abilities from others close to them.

Every Christian leader has an equally pressing responsibility to encourage the development begun by the parent and to make a personal imprint on the life of each child. It is particularly important that the Christian education ministry of the local church, as well as the pastor and staff, recognize and fulfill their obligation as guardians of the potential of every person in their realm of ministry.

Discussion Activities

1. Discuss the purposes of the family as mentioned in the chapter.

2. Share with someone a practical way to teach the meaning of stewardship to your child.

3. What are the gradual steps a family should take to fully implement the "10-70-20 plan"?

4. Discuss how the television advertisers appeal to fantasies of wish fulfillment in our desire for family, intimacy, vitality, and success?

5. In what ways can the Sunday school teacher make a personal imprint on the life of the child?

6

Family Togetherness Activities

BILL GAITHER, SONGWRITER, exhibited accurate insight when he penned these words to a song:*

*We have these moments to hold in our hands
And to touch as they slip thru our fingers like sand.
Yesterday's gone and tomorrow may never come,
But we have these moments today.*

Parents must seize every "teachable moment" they can during each child's formative years for the purpose of communicating Christian values. Even though we are committed to formal instruction of children, research suggests they learn more by observing their parents' lives *informally* every day than by contrived education.

The distinction between formal and informal education in the home is best illustrated in Deuteronomy 6:6, 7 by the command that parents *formally* teach God's words to their children (v. 6) and *informally* talk to them when they sit, walk, recline, and rise each morning (v. 7). This Biblical philosophy of Christian nurture is predicated on the basis that parents model Christian values as a prerequisite to formal instruction in the home.

This is why God has given the great prerequisite, His great warning: "These words . . . shall be on your heart!" Before we can lead our children to love and obey God, we ourselves must be loving and obeying Him (Larry Richards, *You the Parent* [Chicago: Moody Press, 1974], pp. 19, 20).

Family-Night at Home

It is suggested that one evening a week be set aside to strengthen the family unit by engaging in meaningful family activities. What families decide to do will vary from family to family. It should be the family's ultimate purpose not just to encourage lighthearted fun but to inspire spiritual enrichment and wholesome communication.

The proliferation of weeknight activities in the church and society has too often fragmented family relationships. A California congregation is attempting to offset this social imbalance with an emphasis on family night. Pastor Stephen Rexroat states:

> Our midweek service offers all the traditional age-level Bible study and fellowship activities, but we don't call it our family night. We save that title for the one night (Monday) each week set aside to encourage family togetherness.

At the Santa Ana church, no activities are scheduled by members of the staff because they feel family nights should be home nights. Special resource materials are made available to those interested in getting involved in the endeavor.

Objectives of Christian Family Activities

1. To bring a family unit together at regular weekly intervals to enjoy each other's companionship and support.

2. To think about and discuss mutually helpful ideas.

3. To utilize the Bible as a means of finding God's direction for their lives.

4. To express creatively those concepts that form the basis of each week's discussion and activity, and to learn to appreciate each member's contribution.

5. To serve as a sounding board for little problems before they cause serious family divisions.

6. To help each member to develop a stronger sense of self-worth.

7. To help families develop a daily family worship pattern.

8. To provide a friendly supportive group experience for individuals and couples whose present environment may be lonely or threatening to them.

9. To help solidify the framework of marriage by giving couples time to express their love in words and attitudes.

10. To cultivate an active concern for the needs of people outside the family unit—the neighborhood, the community, the world—trying to compass their salvation.

The preceding objectives are featured in the *Christian Family Life Leader's Handbook,* published by Gospel Publishing House, and contained in the *Family Ministry Packet.*

Meaningful in-home activities are *not* parent activities. The primary focus should be on the children and their involvement in the time of sharing. The emphasis should be on life-linked teaching. Everything that is done in the activity time should be practical and applicable to everyday life. Start where you *are* as a family. Christian activities are not just for perfect families. They are for families just like yours. Meaningful family activities should have the following characteristics:

1. *Timing.* Designate a time and place to regularly conduct home activities. Choosing the correct time of day is not as important as conducting activities regularly. Morning? Evening? It depends on your family. The important thing is to find a time when you can get all the family together—a time you can keep. Methods may vary, but it is important to *commit* yourself to one night a week for family night. Whatever is best for *your* family should be the rule.

2. *Brevity.* Try to be brief but not rushed. The activities should be well planned, life relationable, and to the point. Make the theme and objective clear so everyone in the family can understand.

3. *Variety.* Obviously, variety demands creative planning. Keep the activities varied to keep the interest level high. Excellent resources are available from Gospel Publishing House and other sources to assist parents in planning varied activities.

4. *Theme.* Plan a different theme and prayer subject for each activity time. For example, Monday is ready-made for a review of what you learned in church the day before, or prayer time could be devoted to missionaries. Read missionary stories in serial fashion. Correspond with your missionaries by tape

and letter. Your local church can furnish you information on their particular sponsored missionaries. Another day, pray for relatives. Select a theme that is best for the particular time frame your family is in.

5. *Sharing.* There is a lot of talking but not enough communication in most families. Communication demands that the receiver understand what the sender is trying to relate. Since communication is only 7 percent verbal, it is important to be sensitive to tone and body language. Be sensitive to what each family member is trying to say. Give him time to express himself adequately and clearly. A few brief moments of meaningful communication mean more than a week of incessant talking.

6. *Originality.* Activate your creativity when designing your family nights. It is not as difficult as it may seem. The basic requirements for a family night are quite simple. You need a guide, a Scripture passage, and an activity. God's Word is filled with family-night topics. As you unleash the creativity God has given you, your children will be encouraged to do the same.

7. *Teaching Tools.* Find everything you need to make the family activity time more meaningful. Helps such as audiovisuals, cassette recordings, posters, resource books, art, puppets, drama, roleplaying, etc. will make the activity time lively and colorful. Children remember only 10 percent of what they hear, but approximately 90 percent of what they hear, see, say, and do. So involve everyone in hands-on experiences to assure maximum learning.

8. *Informality.* Make the activity child-centered. Parents should avoid being "preachy." Help the younger children understand and participate, so their basic human and spiritual needs will be met.

9. *Planning.* Every member of the family should be able to contribute to planning the activities. A family forum held after the evening meal once or twice a month might be a good time to discuss the idea of planned family activities. A major key to success is involving the children in planning for the events.

Relax! Be sure the home atmosphere will allow for fun and laughter. If the sessions take on an air of heaviness, then postpone or redirect the sharing time. Always avoid a judgmental attitude!

The most crucial factor in the success or failure of the

family-night-at-home activity is the attitudes of parents and children. Recognizing this, parents need to be fully convinced of the value of this learning experience and the potential it holds for each family member's natural and spiritual development.

A Family Affair

A popular, informative in-home activity guide, *The Family Affair*, has been published regularly since the fall 1975. It is designed to encourage parents to capitalize on strengths in family relationships.

The purpose of the guide is to bring the family unit together one night a week for relevant communication and interpersonal sharing among father, mother, and children. Growing relationships depend on constant communication within the home.

Suggestions in the publication for each family night include five categories:

1. Scripture (passage for discussion)
2. Activity Aim (purpose of the evening session)
3. Preparation Tips (list of needed materials)
4. Activity of the Week (suggested get-together activity for the family)
5. Around the Table (mealtime conversation starters)

Highlighting a Biblical passage leads the family to appreciate the fundamental truths taught in the Word of God. More than just reading a particular passage, relating the truth the passage contains to everyday life is the responsibility of the parent. Each activity aim is written in life-relational terms to facilitate maximum learning and to assist parents in teaching.

Recognizing the most effective learning is an involvement process, a family activity is suggested for each week. (It is something the family does together that is desirable, rewarding, exciting, and fun.)

The sample activity that follows is from a past issue of *A Family Affair*.

April 17-23 Recognizing Who I Am

SCRIPTURE Proverbs 3:1-8, *The Living Bible*.

Read the Scripture passage, allowing each family member to read one or two of the sentences.

ACTIVITY AIM

To reinforce in each family member a feeling of recognition of positive traits of personality, appearance, and achievement.

PREPARATION TIPS

1. Check the bulb in your projector or the batteries in your flashlight.
2. Gather white and black paper and chalk.
3. Select your work area for this activity.

ACTIVITY OF THE WEEK

Using a projector or strong flashlight, make silhouettes of each family member. To do this, one parent should hold the light while another outlines the shape of the person who stands between the light and a wall. The shadow of that person should be outlined on black paper with chalk.

The silhouette should then be cut out and mounted on a slightly larger piece of white paper. (You might need to assist younger children with the cutting.) These pictures should be added to the grouping that was started in last week's activity.

"AROUND THE TABLE"

1. Discuss the different physical features of each family member. You might relate which features are inherited from parents and grandparents.
2. Discuss the personality characteristics of each individual and point out any progress that has been made in personality.
3. Emphasize that each person is unique and that God purposely created them differently.
4. Read the Scripture passage again and ask the family to find the character traits a person needs to gain recognition.

The preceding sample activity selected from the quarterly publication would require adaptation to your particular family situation. As with any activity guide, Christian or secular, parents and children must work as a team to apply the experience to their family's position in the family life-cycle.

The ages of the children would be a primary factor in determining the degree of detail for the activity and table discussions. Preschoolers would have different needs from elementary children and teenagers.

Family Worship

The Bible unquestionably values family worship. It instructs parents to "train up a child" (Proverbs 22:6), "teach . . . [their] children" (Deuteronomy 6:7), and raise their children "in the nurture and admonition of the Lord" (Ephesians 6:4).

Parents should be comforted to know the promise of salvation is not only for individuals; it also includes every member of the household! Certainly every parent is encouraged when he reads: "Believe on the Lord Jesus Christ, and thou shalt be saved, *and thy house*" (Acts 16:31). The jailer and his family were saved and received water baptism.

In their excellent guide, *Pray and Play* (pp. 13-22), authors Donald and Nancy Whitehouse reconsider the value of family worship, because it:

1. Strengthens family relationships
2. Aids individual development
3. Follows Biblical pattern for family life
4. Helps parents fulfill their role
5. Teaches children to find meaning in the larger family— the church

The characteristics of family activities already cited in this chapter apply also to family worship. However, there are two factors regarding worship that merit further consideration.

First, the age of the child or children must be considered. The leader must be aware of age differences and learning characteristics. Younger children should not be expected to act "adult." Older children should not be allowed to "put down" younger children. The uninhibited, trusting faith of younger children can teach older children and adults lasting lessons during family worship time.

Second, planning will help set up important boundaries for children. They need to know what is expected of them. They need to know that family worship has a different purpose and is not to be done for an extended time.

In the book *Pray and Play* (pp. 30-34), the authors list what they consider to be essential elements for meaningful family worship:

1. Family members of all ages should participate and contribute
2. Food should be included
3. Games should be included as a means of involving children
4. The Bible is a must
5. Prayer is another essential element for family worship
6. Questions—Unique for family worship
7. Discussion—Another family worship distinctive
8. Time—The most essential element

Today, most of our churches provide extended learning sessions and/or children's church for the younger children during Sunday morning worship. I am excited about these accomplishments in Christian education, but at the same time feel Christian leaders and parents should provide a means to involve their children in periodic worship by:

1. Realizing religious learning is awakened in the child by the end of the first year.
2. Involving the entire children's church in their own worship time.
3. Inviting the children's church into the sanctuary to sit with their families on occasion.
4. Recognizing children are often approached as "spectators" and not allowed to freely participate in children's church activities.
5. Promoting a family concept of worship.
6. Insisting the pastor provide ministry at the child's level of understanding.
7. And, remembering children love pagentry and ritual.

Family Council

Keeping the channels of interpersonal communication open is a primary concern for every Christian parent. Modern family schedules and high levels of television viewing leave the average family little time to talk, least of all, communicate.

To avoid attitude polarization and a communication impasse,

each family should decide on a regular family council for information sharing, discussion, and decisionmaking. Following the parents' lead, family members should agree to participate with an open and transparent point of view.

Leadership in the family council should be provided by a mother-father team with the father taking the leader-moderator role and providing decisions on controversial matters.

The bulk of the discussion and information sharing should be characterized by positive, supportive conversation among family members.

Some areas for discussion during this time might include the following: monthly family calendar, church activities, school activities, family vacation, holiday plans, birthday celebrations, recreation, worship, in-home activities, etc.

Both parents and children will discover that growing together is an exciting adventure as long as family members mutually support one another in love and the fellowship of the Holy Spirit.

Recreation

It is unfortunate that some have gotten the mistaken idea that among Christians if it's enjoyable it must be sinful! This doesn't measure up to what Christ meant when He said: "I am come that they might have life, and that they might have it more abundantly" (John 10:10). If anyone has a right to be joyful it is one who has been *liberated* from sin.

Dig deep into your memory bank and pull from the files some of the incidents that bring the warmest feelings. No doubt you will discover many of the memories relate directly to past recreational events, such as an exciting moment on a family vacation, a frolic on the carpet with your dad, or a ride through the woods on a sunny Sunday afternoon. These were times when an adult stepped down into your childish world or you were invited into theirs. They were times of openness and closeness that are forever etched in your memory.

Many churches are recognizing the need to provide wholesome recreational opportunities for their members and adherents by erecting multipurpose activity buildings for organized sports where families can play together.

Business projections predict recreational equipment will be one of the hottest merchandise areas during the 1980's. Christian leaders and teachers should offer a Christian philosophy of recreation to the body of Christ and to the world.

Rather than making recreation an end in itself, a church in Memphis, Tennessee, has provided a large, carpeted room with a fireplace in their multipurpose building, as a center for families to experience togetherness times after organized recreational events. An age-level graded sports program for individual family members and regular family-oriented events keep the activities building filled with God's joyful, healthy people. Provision is made for outreach to unchurched families in their overall Christian recreational philosophy. And, sister churches in Oklahoma, Alabama, Texas, and other parts of the nation have similar facilities and programs.

What are some of the values of family recreation?

1. It brings all family members to an even plane.
2. It allows children to see parents unencumbered.
3. It gives an occasion for life-relational teaching.
4. It opens channels for interpersonal communication.
5. It helps us apply Scripture to life.
6. It creates an atmosphere for sharing.

What are some family recreational ideas? Why not try some of the following: picnicking, jogging, canoeing, volleyball, table games, singing, walking, archery, gardening, crafts, tennis, cooking, cutting wood, shopping, and camping.

Ask your family what they would like to do. You'll get more suggestions than you can fill. Select the most practical ones and mark them on the calendar.

Discussion Activities

1. List the basic differences implied between formal and informal teaching in the home.

2. In what manner does the family-night-at-home activity fulfill objective #6?

3. Discuss problems that might be encountered by families

who have teenage and preschool children when using *A Family Affair*.

4. What benefits would a regular family council bring to the family?

5. Brainstorm on various ways a family could engage in recreation.

6. Discuss creative approaches to family worship.

7

Developing
Church-family Ministry

TRADITIONALLY, THE SUNDAY SCHOOL has been the leading proponent of nurture and enrichment for the family. Today, that is the case more than ever. However, the church, with its primary leadership (the pastor, staff, deacons, etc.) along with the Christian education department, should move more vigorously into the limelight, leading the call for renewed ministry to this vital institution—the family.

With this principle in mind, I want to focus primarily on the church's responsibility to develop family ministry. Our purpose in promoting family ministries should be to enrich and enable each person to reach his maximum potential for Christ.

Where Do We Begin?

It is impossible to *start* a family ministry. Why? Because every church and Sunday school *already* is ministering to families to some degree. However, one can *expand* and *improve* this vital Christian education ministry to meet more needs.

A family ministry is not something you just add to the regular church programs. It must be integrated throughout the entire church ministry. You are ministering to families when: you add a family elective to the curriculum, you help a widow or divorced person, you visit the elderly, or you give advice to a couple about to be married.

Family ministry is more than programs and events that focus on family life. It is a church life-style in which individuals are equipped and encouraged to live in harmony together in their homes.

79

Family ministry is also church leaders modeling with their own families the principles that help build successful homes. It is ministry whereby families in units and individual family members are given the opportunity to develop fully into the life-style of Jesus Christ. It is ministry that enables family members to relate effectively to others in expressing their personal Christian faith.

With this definition of family ministry in view, it would be reasonable to assume the ability of churches and Sunday schools to achieve a *model* family ministry is widely varied.

PHILOSOPHY

Why should the church develop a family ministry? The magnitude of a family ministry is seemingly overwhelming. Family life-styles have been entrenched by generations of living, therefore, the problems of family relationships are usually deep and numerous.

How Leaders Approach This Issue

Already churches are concerned with missions, Bible study, evangelism, discipling, worship, Christian education, church growth, etc. Family-life education is one more duty added to an already overburdened schedule.

To answer the question: "Why should the church develop family ministry?" we reiterate current factors of family fragmentation in our society, including:

—over half the labor force is women
—educational institutions portray the role of wife and mother as passé
—families are constantly on the move
—negative influence of television viewing on family interaction
—steady rise in violent crime
—failure to control sexual impulses (teenage pregnancies have increased 33 percent within last 5 years)
—increased incidence of homosexuality and also much freedom in expressing it

Historically, among churches, there has been a tendency toward the *either-or* philosophy—to focus on *either* the church *or* the home. For example, churches known for their large memberships are not, by and large, also known for a strong focus on the family.

This either-or complex is due in part to a history of competition for the resources of the persons who "run the church." The faithful workers are so heavily involved that their family relationships pay the price and their children are robbed of what is rightfully theirs. At the other extreme are those who have become so family-oriented they decline to serve, citing their need to spend time with the family.

Somewhere between the two extremes, leaders try to meet the challenge by token emphases such as a yearly family week, a family night, or premarital counseling sessions before a wedding. This partial approach lacks continuity and will not develop strong homes. The church must lay plans to enrich the homes at *every level,* and this may require radical surgery on the church's philosophy, schedule, and programming.

Still other churches hesitate to "come on strong" for the family because they see this ministry as excluding singles in the congregation. They fail to see that the New Testament concept of the family provides wholeness for singles who are also members of family units.

There needs to be a declaration of an intent to unite by the church and the home. To continue some current philosophies will only prolong the agony and make future reconciliation more difficult. The home continues to fragment while Christian leaders and parents are deliberating!

Biblical Foundations for Family Ministry

Family ministry is not a fad or trend that we expose ourselves to in order to be "in." It is Biblical in its foundation and inception.

In the Old Testament, family living is defined: God builds the family (Psalm 127); husbands and wives are to become one (Genesis 2:24); parents are to teach godly values to their children (Deuteronomy 6:4-9) and to discipline them (Proverbs

19:18); and children are to obey and honor their parents (Proverbs 1:8; Exodus 20:12).

The New Testament teaches husbands to love their wives (Colossians 3:19); the oneness of husband and wife is reemphasized (Ephesians 5:31, 33); and children are to be brought up in the discipline and instruction of the Lord (6:4) and they are to obey their parents (6:1-3). A primary qualification for an elder or deacon within the church family is that he manages his own household well (1 Timothy 3:4, 12).

There are relatively few passages that speak directly to family life. However, even though Scripture only briefly outlines principles of family living, many passages directed to the church also apply to the home. In the early stages of Christianity, the home *was* the church (1 Corinthians 16:15). What was written to the church was also written to individual families. Most of the New Testament, then, can be applied directly to individual family units.

Implications for Family Ministry

The implications for family ministry are obvious. Like the church, the "church in miniature," the family, also grows properly when each part is functioning in love. When the members are not functioning properly within the home, the church is adversely affected, for the church is comprised mainly of families. Christian leaders and teachers should reevaluate their present ministry to families and, if needed, expand their perimeters by meeting more family needs.

The message a local body communicates to and about the family is conveyed more by what it *does* than by what it *says*. Our philosophy is seen in what we *do* more than what we *say*. Long-term involvement in building Christian families should be the primary task of the church and Sunday school. Review the supportive functions of the body to the family mentioned in chapter 2.

ORGANIZATION

There are no "typical" churches or organizational structures, so each leader should design his own procedures. However, the priorities suggested on the next page should be followed.

1. *Share Concerns.* The pastor should share his concerns with the church leadership because they need to recognize family ministry as a high-priority need before an acceptable outreach to families can be accomplished. If only a few people get involved the chances of success are minimal.

Leaders should model Biblical principles of family life in their own home as a prerequisite to success with other families.

The pastor should personally meet with his board, members of the Christian education committee, teachers, and leaders before he talks to the congregation. Since some will see this as a threat to "regular" church programs, the leader will need to show that competition need not exist and strong families will make a strong church.

To arouse interest and concern for families, you will need to enlist a group of people to study the family needs of your congregation.

2. *Select Family Committee.* Set up a family-life committee. The size and characteristics of your group will be determined by the size of your church, etc.

Committee members should be committed to their own families. They should be practicing Christian principles of family living and should have a desire to help other families.

Avoid appointing people who are already loaded down with church responsibilities. If you must select someone already heavily involved, ask him to voluntarily shift some of his work load to others who aren't so involved.

Select a committee that represents a wide variety of needs and interests. You will need members with children of varied ages; representatives from the elderly, single, widowed, divorced, and middle-aged; representatives from all auxiliary functions (Royal Rangers, Women's Ministries, etc.). Also, involve someone from the official board.

3. *Appoint a Family-life Coordinator.* He should be chairman of the family-life committee and work directly under the pastor. The best move would be to hire a full-time staff member and give him authority to direct meaningful family ministries throughout the entire church program. Churches unable to hire a full-time person could appoint a lay person to serve in this capacity.

The job description for the family-life coordinator should include the following: correlate family activities in the church, encourage family activities at home, develop the quality of family life, provide information on family relationships and nurture, encourage financial responsibility, and suggest seminars, curriculum, discussions, etc.

4. *Determine Family Needs.* A comprehensive survey should be made. Three methods include observation, surveys, and general family information. Select the best approach suited to your church and Sunday school.

After this information is gathered, have the family committee review the findings and arrange the needs by order of priority. Now you are ready to identify key purposes for family ministry in your congregation.

5. *Establish Purposes for Ministry.* Purposes are based on the needs determined in the congregational survey. When you establish a purpose, you are stating a direction for your ministry; you are stating an aim that will help meet specific goals (i.e., to help families communicate more effectively).

6. *Set Goals.* Goals will enable you to meet your purposes. The goals should be specific ones that can be both measured and accomplished.

The example given earlier in the chapter, to help families communicate effectively, could be approached through the following goals: conduct a class on communication for parents, teach a similar section to teens, and bring parents and teens together for an in-depth seminar.

Goal setting involves planning definite activities. It would be wise to set short- and long-range goals. Even though you may have to change your goals, project ministry into the future.

7. *Make Plans.* Ask: How will we reach our goals? Who will be responsible? When will we reach our goals?

Great ideas often die for lack of follow-through. Hard work and planning are needed to realize a meaningful ministry to families.

8. *Evaluate Your Goals.* Keeping an obsolete program going long after it has fulfilled its usefulness minimizes effectiveness. Expect each expressed goal to meet the evaluation

test: Did our plan help us meet our purpose? What changes do we need to make to be more effective in the future?

This evaluation feedback exercise will help you see to whom you have ministered and to what extent you have met families' needs.

DEVELOPMENT

Now that we have looked at philosophy and the steps for organization, it would be advisable to consider two critical factors in developing a family ministry.

It takes *time* to build an effective ministry to families. Attempting shortcuts will not create a solid base of operation. Many good ideas fall by the way because leaders are not patient and rush unprepared into supposedly foolproof programs.

Qualified Leaders

It is imperative that you train qualified leaders to assist you in implementing successful family ministries. It is recommended that you select a core of potential leaders and initiate a methodical training program with them.

Search the body for believers who have a distinct interest and spiritual inclination toward family ministry. You may have to rely on your intuition at first but time will reveal whether the candidate is the person God wants for this outreach. Seek also to identify parents, teachers, and leaders who exhibit spiritual gifts of leadership and who project deep concern for family needs. If there is some hesitancy on a worker's part after he launches into the training, allow him to withdraw at his own initiative.

Training should include reading in a specific area of family concern; attending church-directed leadership classes; participating in a training event; and experimenting with the concepts in one's own home and family. Potential leaders should be encouraged to attend seminars and family-related events locally and nationally.

Tie in to Existing Programs

A second imperative to developing family ministry is to tie in to existing programs. "New ventures" are more favorably received by church and Sunday school leaders when they are seen as part of an already functioning unit. A strong Sunday program or adult class could be an effective vehicle for introducing some aspect of family-life education.

IMPLEMENTATION

Avoid trying to do too much your first year. It is better to enlarge your ministry to families at a more gradual pace. Select several well-thought-out goals for your first year, do a thorough job with these, then evaluate and plan your strategy for the next year(s).

Goals to attempt the first year might include one or all of the following. A more detailed description of the ministries briefly mentioned below can be found in chapters 6 and 9.

Marriage-Enrichment Retreat

A marriage retreat is a very rewarding experience for couples and a logical beginning point for family enrichment. A Friday through Sunday noon experience discussing topics like communication, roles, foundations, and conflict resolution would enrich family life immeasurably.

Family Night-at-Home

Structuring a certain night every week with no church activities and designating it as family home night would nurture family life in the congregation.

Caution! Parents must be trained to initiate family times by observing a model family-at-home experience. This could be done in a Sunday school class or in the midweek or Sunday night service. Curriculum and instructions should be provided to assure meaningful in-home Christian activities.

Parenting Class

The young-married Sunday school class could set aside a quarter and focus on major parenting issues like discipline, values, communication, worship, stewardship, etc., to improve the members' ability as Christian parents.

In conclusion, two factors need to be reiterated. First, the best approach for the church and Sunday school would be to pilot a program with a select group before involving the entire congregation. Organizational research with families and churches underscores the need to fully examine a new concept of ministry to determine if an idea adequately meets the needs for which it has been designed. Second, earnestly seek the direction of the Holy Spirit in implementing various aspects of family ministry.

Discussion Activities

1. What are the church's and Sunday school's responsibilities to the family?

2. What is the family's responsibility to the church and Sunday school?

3. List the first three steps the leader should take to implement family ministry in the church and in the Sunday school?

4. Who should make up the family-life committee?

5. Briefly discuss the three family-related programs suggested for the first year.

8

Reaching Every Family Member

OUR SOCIETY IS IN A STATE OF TRANSITION. Single adults make up a large—and growing—part of America's population. The starting point for the church and the Sunday school in reaching every family member—divorced, single, or senior—is *preventive* and *enriching* ministry to the family. From there we move into special ministries to each social group.

SINGLE ADULTS

The 1977 U.S. Statistical Abstract revealed a high percentage of single adults in America. Since this is a rapidly expanding social group, it will be helpful for churches and teachers to analyze who makes up the social groups in their church or class. A survey should be conducted to classify by percentages the makeup of the social structure. For example, the statistical abstract revealed:

Single parent, female (one or more children)	6.2%
Single parent, male (one or more children)	0.6%
Single-person households	20.6%
Married couple (with no children at home)	30.5%
Father wage earner and mother homemaker (with one or more children)	15.9%
Father wage earner and mother wage earner (with one or more children)	18.5%

Unrelated couple living together	2.5%
Female- or male-headed households	5.3%
(that include relatives other	
than spouses or children)	

This information shows the expanding challenge of ministry to single adults. It is imperative that every Christian leader become aware of all prospects who are single. Generally, 20 to 30 percent of adult church membership will be single.

Single adults have varied expectations so openly receive them into an atmosphere of acceptance and into a learning experience that meets them at their point of need.

Needs

Single adults come to a particular church or class because of specific needs. Some of the basic needs of single adults are for: acceptance, increased self-worth, help in fighting loneliness, companionship, financial assistance, help in managing their children, understanding, and knowing God's will for their lives.

If the Christian teacher can find a direct approach to a single's need and then meet that need, he will probably win that person as a friend. This approach will work successfully with anyone, single or not.

Organization

Let the group decide on a name for themselves. Encourage them to select a positive name that connotes Christian action and growth.

Grouping

Garden Grove Community Church groups their singles in four autonomous groups: *Pacesetters* are in their twenties; *Innovators* are in their thirties; *Motivators* are in their forties; and *Lamplighters* are over 50. The age groupings give each age-range its own identity, interest levels, and single-parent age-range, and there is a similarity of problems encountered.

A large church in Seattle, Washington, has three main groups designated by age called FOCAS I (ages over 45); MID-FOCAS (ages 35-45); and FOCAS II (ages under 35).

Location

When organizing a group you might find it advisable to conduct your meetings at a local restaurant or home on Sunday mornings. Locating the meetings away from the church will attract outside singles and free church singles from inhibitions. The meetings should be conducted early enough for singles who choose to become part of the morning worship service. It is important that the church let the singles know they are welcomed and accepted. Most of them are searching for alternatives to the swinging social life of their peers. Your church, Bible-study group, or Sunday school class can be that alternative.

Committees

The leader should appoint the necessary committees for ministry functions, including: music, program, publicity, membership, outreach, fellowship (social), spiritual life, now-help, and family life.

Finance

The sponsoring church will need to subsidize the program until it becomes self-supporting. Records of contributions, gifts, and offerings should be kept for income tax purposes. A functional bookkeeping system will greatly assist in keeping all financial obligations promptly paid. It is recommended the group regularly support home and foreign missions projects whenever possible.

Creative Bible Study

Singles like to be involved in weekly Bible-study classes. Include your adults in the learning process; involve them in exploring God's Word and in discovering how Biblical truths apply to their individual lives. Encourage class members to make positive life changes based on principles they discover in Scripture.

Evaluation

When establishing a new ministry for singles, it will be necessary to maintain a clear perspective by keeping the communication channels open in both directions. Keep in touch with singles through questionnaires, conversation, discussion groups, open meetings, and evaluation forms. Ask for their opinions and reactions to each new addition and deletion from the program. As this new ministry matures, the need for evaluation is less critical than in the beginning. However, there will always be the need for feedback from the singles group.

Leadership

Selecting the right leader is probably the most important decision you will make when beginning a singles group. The leader need not be single, but he/she must have a positive attitude toward singles and Christian life. A husband/wife team is suggested for your initial leadership. Seek God's guidance in securing individuals who have perfected their gifts of administration, leadership, and teaching. Make sure the leader's personal life is above reproach.

Since you will be involving singles outside the church, it would be best to require that your *primary* leaders be regular members of the church congregation. Limit secondary leadership (such as committee members, etc.) to 6-month terms, with no limits on the director if he has an effective ministry.

Properly trained leaders are imperative for successful singles groups. Plan a 2-day singles leadership retreat. Share a comprehensive overview of the program and invite feedback and discussion on basic issues.

Plan annually to send your primary leadership to a training seminar. A singles leadership seminar was held in Seattle, Washington, last winter with over 1,000 in attendance. Write FOCAS, Calvary Temple, 6810 Eighth Avenue N.E., Seattle, WA 98115, for details.

Caring

The singles program should be characterized by a warm and accepting environment for everyone who attends. Plan by appointing a caring coordinator for the singles class. This person exhibits love and concern for members and visitors by maintaining regular, close contact by phone calls, visits, and postcards. He encourages members to participate in Sunday school, worship services, church activities, socials, and special projects. He visits the sick and absentees, and communicates their needs to the teacher.

Get Started

Each new singles ministry grows one step at a time and by trial and error. Avoid trying to reach the top step in the first jump. Ask experienced leaders for helpful advice and ideas. Research what other churches are doing; visit their programs and talk to their leaders. Identify pitfalls and avoid known problem areas. Plan together. If you have a small group of singles, join with other churches for fellowship and information sharing. Cultivate an interchurch group which meets quarterly and grows together, yet allows singles to function at various levels in their own church.

Church Relationships

If single adults are going to be the church, then the ministry of the church should be *with* singles and not *for* singles.

Most churches approach their ministry to singles by trying to fit them into the married-adult program. Single adults need to be integrated into the total ministry of the body, just as any other adults. Therefore, we must minister to singles as a special-need group and as an integral part of the church.

SENIOR ADULTS

One-third of the present total membership of many church congregations is past the age of 65. By the turn of the century one-third of the U.S. population will be senior adults. As people age, they undergo emotional and psychological changes. Studies indicate that teenagers and people over 60 are most open to change. Local church members interested in new forms of worship usually are under 25 or over 60. Statistics tell us the U.S. family currently spans 4½ generations, and is on the threshold of 5.

You can have a meaningful ministry with the senior adults in your class, church, and community. These guidelines are presented to help you develop a ministry with the largest single minority in this country.

The Potential for a Program

If the church is to effectively mobilize its resources to accomplish its tasks of evangelism and spiritual maturity, it must consciously involve its senior adults.

Ideally, of course, senior adults will have already been involved in the church's ministry, so when they have more time available, they will continue and even increase their involvement. But how do you set a program in motion when not all senior adults are active, for whatever reason? Here are some suggestions.

Senior Adult Needs

A survey of senior adults has pinpointed the following basic needs, ranked in terms of importance by those who responded:

1. To be loved and appreciated
2. To do a useful, significant job
3. To be accepted and respected as a group
4. To gain information about money (wills)
5. To secure health information
6. To meet transportation needs
7. To have counselors to talk with
8. To have recreational activities

Keep in mind these needs as you plan your ministry to the senior adults in your class, congregation, and community. Add to them the spiritual concerns, often unarticulated but real, and seek ways to meet them.

When Senior Adults Need You

Not all senior adults are able to participate in an active program. And even those who are active have special needs the church can meet. Often they are lonely. Families scatter. Friends die. Incomes are limited. They are concerned about the future. Life can become drab at times, because of physical limitations. They need someone to love, and someone who will love and appreciate them. They need recognition and respect. They need good friends. They need the spiritual help and renewal that Christian fellowship in prayer and service can bring.

On the practical side, some need financial advice and health information. Those in charge of a senior-adult group should be well-informed concerning community services available, and help the members take advantage of these.

Planning Together

Begin by surveying the members to ascertain the nature of senior-adult ministry needed in your church. Invite all who are "55 and better" to complete a questionnaire indicating their needs, interests, and abilities. While 55 is not retirement age, an increasing number of people are aware that fruitful retirement begins with preparation in the middle years.

Appoint a Committee

Appoint a committee to study the results of the survey, along with any other information available about the senior adults in your church and community.

The committee should include the pastor or appointed representative; leaders of the Sunday school, youth group, men's department, and women's ministries; and a couple representing senior adults. All groups already involved in ministry with or to senior adults should also be represented on the committee.

Hear From the Senior Adult

Before determining the type of senior-adult program the church will launch, the pastor should call a meeting of all the senior adults and have a discussion as to what they would like to do. They may choose to be a special-interest group and to confirm a couple as their leaders. This couple, working closely with a staff member appointed by the pastor, would have responsibility for arranging special events for senior adults.

The church staff member assigned to work with the senior-adult leaders will serve as a liaison between the senior adults and all departments of the church; finding ways for the various departments to help the group, or individuals in need, and (more often) ways the senior adults may contribute to the ministry of the departments.

Members of the church can help senior adults by organizing youth, men, and women teams to:

—visit shut-ins regularly
—provide transportation for church and shopping
—adopt a "grandmother" or "grandfather"
—listen
—provide a telephone ministry of concern
—provide extension Bible classes when needed
—provide tapes of services
—provide large-print Bibles when needed

Ministry to Senior Adults

The type of senior-adult program the church develops will depend on the nature of the senior-adult group and their most urgent needs.

Ministry With Senior Adults

A little direction or encouragement from the pastor can start senior adults on a meaningful ministry. Give retired persons a job they can do, and you will bless both them and the church. Consider how they could help in areas where their skills may now be largely unused:

—as telephone operators
—as carpenters
—as counselors
—in preparing visual aids
—in assisting new converts
—in visiting the unchurched
—in outreach to senior citizens groups

—in visiting shut-ins

—in contacting newcomers

Senior adults can perform most of the tasks younger members can and, as a rule, they have more time to become involved.

An exciting new realm of ministry for senior adults is supportive ministries in the Sunday school classroom. Although largely unexplored, this opportunity will be eagerly grasped by senior adults who have been standing on the sidelines. Leaders should invite them into the action as: nursery workers to cuddle little babies; preschool assistants for routine tasks; elementary guides in learning-center activities; youth chaperones and counselors; and adult teachers and assistants. These are but a few of the possibilities for utilizing the great reservoir of wisdom and experience inherent in our senior citizens.

Activities for Senior Adults

Senior adults now have time for many activities they had to forego in their busier years. Many of them find they enjoy planning activities with those who have common interests, such as weekday programs of social activities, adult education, and handcrafts. They also find cultural activities and service projects very stimulating. For example, they can attend daytime meetings more readily than those with heavier responsibilities.

Here are a few social activities they will enjoy: attending fellowship meetings, daytime prayer groups and Bible studies, sharing potluck lunches together, hobbies, church bus trips, picnics, and special projects for the church. (Thanks to Silas Gaither, director of Church Ministries, and the Senior Adult Committee members who contributed information for this chapter segment.)

DIVORCED ADULTS

Today divorce is occurring at an alarming rate, even among Christian families.

The number of divorces compared with marriages was one divorce for every six marriages in 1940. Twenty years later, in 1960, it was almost one in four. By 1970, it was almost one in three. Now, the spiraling trend leads us near the rate of one divorce for every marriage.

Only a few years ago it was taboo to even talk about divorce, but now many people who are becoming Christians have already suffered through divorce proceedings. And, many divorcees are reaching out for comfort and forgiveness in Christ, becoming members, and worshiping alongside other Christians.

Historically, divorce has been one of the most difficult issues for Christians to face and, consequently, there is a two-sided attitudinal problem that needs to be dealt with.

Many Christians mistakenly "label" most divorced persons as "unacceptable" and shy away from granting them full acceptance. On the other hand, divorced persons are very sensitive to ostracism and usually avoid projecting themselves in their new identity.

As Christian leaders, we need to face this issue head-on and reevaluate our attitude toward divorcees and their families. Jesus set the example for forgiveness when He stood between the scribes and Pharisees and the woman taken in adultery (John 8:7).

We need to understand the extreme period of adjustment required by an abrupt change in life-style. Both men and women who suffer divorce struggle daily with unmet needs, loneliness, and a sense of failure.

Divorced adults and their children need the supportive environment of the church and nurture from concerned Christians to begin the healing process from the deep psychological scars and taxing physical traumas caused by marital upheaval. Consideration should be given to answering, as much as possible, the spiritual questions generated by separation. Even though we might know some of the facts about the situation, we must avoid placing blame and encourage the divorced person to live each day to the fullest, knowing God forgives all sin. Even though divorce is a crisis, it is not synonymous with disaster.

Since it is the children who are most affected by divorce, we need to: become aware of their feelings, reach out to comfort them, learn to be more patient, and encourage them with positive words. We should involve them in class projects and assignments, and recognize the need to remain stable and exhibit love and understanding, especially during the critical phase of the divorce proceedings.

SINGLE PARENTS

Regardless of the circumstances we live in, we each are a necessary part of the body of Christ (1 Corinthians 12:12, 21-26). No individual part of the Body can exist outside a constant vital link with other Body members. We are all important; we all need each other.

Although God forgives the mistakes of the past, single parents have to live with the natural consequences of those mistakes. Even those who may not be primarily at fault will have to face the results for time to come.

Some practical guidelines and suggestions for assisting single parents are:

1. Encourage senior citizens and children of single parents to establish meaningful relationships.

2. Provide time for regular families to interact with single parents and their children.

3. Allow single parents to get together regularly to share and care with other single parents.

4. Help youth become involved in helpful projects to provide assistance in daily matters.

5. Direct singles to knowledgeable members in the congregation who can wisely counsel and advise them.

6. Staff the nursery and Sunday school with both men and women to enable children from single-parent homes to have contact with both father and mother substitutes.

7. Circulate a questionnaire to determine which adults want to lend special assistance to single-parent families.

Discussion Activities

1. What approach do you suggest to determine the number of single adults in your church, class, and community? How can you contact them most effectively?

2. List the reasons why single adults flow in and out of class.

3. How can we integrate more senior adults into the Christian education program?

4. Discuss the attitudes of church members toward the divorced and the attitude of the divorcee toward the church.

5. What effects does divorce have on the children? How can Christian teachers deal with these influences?

9
Exciting
Family Ministry

THE GREATEST RESERVOIR OF CHRISTIAN LEADERSHIP is the Christian home. By far more people are saved as elementary children than at any other age. Christian leaders need to view every family member as a potential person to help expand the kingdom of God.

Even though we appreciate and rely heavily on our highly trained, experienced, and dedicated pastoral leadership, we must issue the challenge, as Christ did, for *everyone* to get involved in the propagation of the gospel! It is, by and large, to be a volunteer army of believers. The apostle Paul clearly outlines the concept whereby divinely ordained leaders are to perfect the *saints* "for the *work* of the ministry" (Ephesians 4:12).

The pattern in the Book of Acts was sharing the message from house to house (Acts 2). This first-century proven method is equally successful today in churches worldwide. For example, the phenomenal church in Seoul, Korea, pastored by Dr. Cho, is a modern-day example of the New Testament principle. Hundreds of home cell-groups have swelled that body of believers to over 100,000!

Training and Outreach

This chapter will describe several outstanding family-oriented methods currently being used in Christian education circles.

These methods are listed on the next page.

The training/outreach classifications are not intended to be

101

restrictive but are suggested to support the concept of balance between ministry to the body and to the world. The possibilities of family-enrichment ministries are limited only by our imaginations!

Training	*Outreach*
Christian Parenting Class	Family Happening
Family-Enrichment Services	Family-Enrichment Conference
Family Clustering	
Marriage-Enrichment Retreat	

CHRISTIAN PARENTING CLASS

Every parent needs help in parenting! The Sunday school can extend a helping hand by providing a regular class for existing and prospective parents.

The purpose of the class should be to assist parents in daily parenting tasks through applied practical and Biblical principles. Attention should be focused on basic family structure and successfully fulfilling parental responsibilities.

Basic considerations for initiating the class include the following:

1. Proper class leadership is a crucial factor. A parent leader-couple would work most effectively. The lead couple must exhibit practical and spiritual maturity.

2. The main resource for this suggested class should be the Bible even though it does not purport to be a textbook on parenting. Other texts should be used as a curriculum so long as they are true to Biblical principles and up-to-date. Two outstanding texts are: *The Christ-Centered Family* by Raymond Brock (Springfield, MO: Gospel Publishing House, 1977), and *The Family First* by Kenneth Gangel (Minneapolis: HIS International Service). Also, check the resource guide at the end of each chapter.

3. Since students learn best when involved in their own

learning, the instructor-couple should read Ron Held's *Learning Together* (Springfield, MO: Gospel Publishing House, 1976), as a prerequisite to teaching the class. A variety of methods should be used to create excitement and motivate students to learn. Audiovisuals should be used including films, slides, filmstrips, and an overhead projector. Prepare worksheets and give frequent homework activities and assignments. Ask successful parents from the church body to share their parental experience in class.

4. Encourage parents to apply the basic concepts discussed in class to their own attitudes and family relationships. Disallow in class the betrayal of intimate family confidences and problems. Out-of-class appointments and telephone contacts may work best in sensitive matters.

5. Suggested topics for the class include: authority and relationships, training, outside influences on the family, causes of misbehavior among children, home and church cooperation, recreation and leisure, discipline, human sexuality, finances, spiritual development of the child, preparation for marriage, and communication.

6. A good subject area to begin the class is basic principles for a growing marital relationship. Introduce the group to enrichment concepts shared by Norman Wright's two excellent volumes, *The Pillars of Marriage* and *Communication: Key to Your Marriage* (Glendale, CA: Gospel Light/Regal Books).

FAMILY-ENRICHMENT CONFERENCE

A family-enrichment conference should be used as one of several approaches in family-life ministry. It will be more effective when used in connection with other emphases throughout the year rather than as a "one-shot" approach by itself.

(Since there are many similarities between the family-enrichment conference and the family-enrichment leadership seminar described later in this chapter, attention will be given to details not covered in that chapter section.)

Purpose

The purpose of the family-enrichment conference is to provide an environment where information can be received, new insights developed, and positive action taken to enrich the home life of the participants.

It should not be perceived as a clinic for sick families or group therapy for quarreling couples. Rather, it is a way of enhancing good relationships that already exist. Hopefully, the environment in the conference will be supportive so each participant can be open and honest in the sharing periods. It should create a desire for change and give participants knowledge on how changes can be achieved.

Planning

Proper planning will mean the difference between success and failure. This should include purchasing and preparing resource materials, training leadership, and securing supportive help. A guest speaker and perhaps one or more resource persons should be included.

Survey Family Needs

First, survey family needs. Methods for taking this survey include a questionnaire, individual interviews, or group discussion. A printed survey form seems to work best. Assist participants in registering their feelings: strongly agree, mildly agree, undecided, mildly oppose, strongly oppose. Provide additional blank space for suggestions.

In an information-gathering session, questions and group discussions should be written ahead of time with parents, teens, and children asked to voluntarily participate in the meeting.

A discussion group could be formed by the pastor, staff, board members, and representatives from all ministries in the church including: Sunday school, Missionettes, Royal Rangers, women's ministries, youth, etc. Also, include in the discussion various types of family units, such as retired adults, single parents, families with teens, families with small children, childless couples, etc.

Set Goals

After determining the major needs, set achievable goals for

different age and interest groups including: retired adults, adults in their middle years, parents with teenagers, parents of preteens, young-married adults, never-married adults, formerly married singles, premarital adults, teenagers, and children.

Even though there are many possibilities in grouping adults by age, you may want to start with fewer groupings. Or, you may prefer to group adults by interest or subjects. Whichever you choose, adults will benefit most when they openly discuss their own problems.

Methods

Use methods that will accomplish the goals you have set. These may range from a minilecture to creative activities. It is important to remember that children, youth, and adults learn best when they are directly involved and when they have to make decisions based on life experiences or case studies.

In addition to Ron Held's *Learning Together,* there are four excellent age-level handbooks (preschool, elementary, youth, and adult) available from Gospel Publishing House that could be consulted for creative methodology ideas.

Format

The schedule for the family-enrichment conference should be based on what will work best for your church.

The program will function best if you ask everyone to meet in the auditorium for an opening session (30 minutes), break up into study groups (1 hour), then return to the auditorium for feedback and worship (30 minutes).

Leadership

Securing qualified leadership is the most important factor in the success of the conference. Each person offering assistance should be adequately trained for his/her assigned topic or responsibility. Involve senior adults, single adults, parents of different age-groups, ministers, and community resource people. Leaders should feel comfortable with their subject and make others feel comfortable as well. Before you begin be sure everyone is thoroughly briefed on the purpose and details of the meeting.

Publicity

This is an excellent opportunity to reach people outside your church. Promote the conference within the church by posters, church mailings, bulletin inserts, announcements, and skits. To promote it outside the church, use newspaper advertisements, newsstories, television announcements, radio, and community bulletins.

Followup

A regular family-night-at-home should be scheduled by participating families following the conference. This conference affords the opportunity to underscore the need for fun and worship activities within the home. Chapter 6 contains information on this type of family ministry.

Evaluation

Soon after the meeting, evaluate whether or not the conference goals have been reached. An evaluation sheet should be used with a rating scale to indicate the degree of accomplishment.

The church staff should review all information received after the conference and make future projections for family-related ministries. Catalog this information for future planning.

FAMILY HAPPENING

Often ministers share their feelings that the church is not bridging the gap to nurture and enrich families facing dilemmas. Society in general and families in particular are reaching out for someone to share Christian fellowship and counsel on a person-to-person basis.

An Illinois pastor asked if I could help him with a program that would inform and inspire his church families and at the same time reach out to the unsaved in the community.

He was concerned that activity in his church had become too

platform-oriented. He said: "Recent revivals, though well-financed and attended, seemingly brought few results. I want to depart from some of the things I have leaned on for progress in the past; try something different for a change."

I described to him my plan for a family-oriented revival called a "Family Happening." This is one example of the family-enrichment conference. He decided to schedule one for his church and invited me to be with him for the event.

The Christian education committee, led by the pastor, began preparations for the "Family Happening" by decorating the foyer and the church sanctuary.

Kickoff

The four-night "Family Happening" began with a Sunday morning message reviewing "Our Christian Heritage." Sunday evening the pastor continued the challenge to parents and asked each family to sign a statement pledging to attend the services faithfully with their children and to renew their dedication by increasing Christian nurture in their homes. They were also encouraged to invite neighboring families to attend the "Family Happening."

Program

The time each evening was divided into three segments:

I. *Action Time*

During the opening 20 minutes, everyone age 6 and above met in the sanctuary for lively choruses, theme promotion, progress reporting, and brief Scripture games. The primary purpose of the opening was to focus attention on the purpose of the "Family Happening."

II. *Discovery Groups*

For 1 hour, the participants met in various groups including:
A. Elementary (6-12)
B. Youth (13-17)
C. Single Adults
D. Senior Adults
E. Parent Clinic

III. *Family Worship*

Following the discovery-group time, everyone returned to the main auditorium for Bible study, inspiration, and worship. Several families were asked to highlight the services with a special family feature.

Short action games, purposely involving participants with considerable age differences, encouraged healthy competition between the generations. Care was taken to insure that everyone got involved!

The Bible message was simple and to the point. Families were encouraged to sit and worship together.

Results

Since it was an innovative approach to revival and the church had never attempted a family emphasis like this, we distributed response sheets to the participants.

Some of the members were so impressed, they suggested that succeeding midweek services be changed to conform to the special-emphasis format.

FAMILY-ENRICHMENT LEADERSHIP SEMINAR

The purpose of this leadership seminar is to sensitize church leadership to the need for nurture and enrichment for the family; to instruct them on basic issues and influences; to discuss the areas of conflict between the church and the home; and to explore new and exciting areas of family ministry.

(This seminar is similar to the family-enrichment conference described earlier in this chapter. This seminar, the marriage-enrichment retreat, and the "Family Happening" have many similarities in learning, methodology, promotion, and publicity. Refer to those sections for greater detail.)

Bring your entire church leadership together including: pastors; church staff; board members; Sunday school superintendents; teachers; men's, women's, and children's ministry directors; etc. Also, include representatives from youth, senior adults, singles, and various types of family structures. (This is the family committee already mentioned in chapter 7.)

Necessary subjects for discussion should include:
—Issues facing families today
—Outside influences on the Christian home
—Types of families
—Basic scriptural foundations of marriage and family life
—Family goals
—How to conduct a family survey
—Church and home relationships
—How to develop a family ministry
—Family-life programs

The basic difference between the family-enrichment leadership seminar and the family-enrichment conference is the seminar is primarily oriented toward church leadership, while the conference is directed toward parents. One seeks to inspire family enrichment through the ministry of the local church; the other attempts to support parents in practical everyday living.

The primary goal of the family-enrichment leadership seminar is to encourage the addition of a family-life coordinator to the church ministerial staff (as mentioned in chapter 7). It would be best if this person were a full-time minister. A second option would be to select an outstanding lay person to serve in this capacity. He should be experienced in family matters and highly respected by the church and community.

His major job responsibility should involve supervision of the overall family ministry of the church, in direct association with the pastor and other church leaders. He should chair the family-life committee, representing all areas of ministry in the church.

FAMILY CLUSTERING

The family cluster model came into being in 1970; since then it has become the best-known form of family enrichment in churches of all faiths and denominations throughout the North American continent. Margaret M. Sawin, founder of the model, writes:

A family cluster is a group of four or five complete family units which contract to meet together periodically over an extended period of time for shared educational experiences related to their living in relationship within their families. A cluster provides mutual support, training in skills which facilitates the family living in relationship, and celebration of their life and beliefs together *(Family Enrichment With Family Clusters* [Valley Forge, PA: Judson Press, 1979], p. 27).

The basic goals of the family cluster model are:

1. To provide an intergenerational group of family units where children can relate easily to adults and adults to children.

2. To provide a group which can grow in support and mutuality for its members.

3. To provide a group where parents and children can gain perspective about each other in contact with other parents and children.

4. To provide an opportunity for families to consider experiences they deem important.

5. To provide a group in which families can model for each other communication, decisionmaking, problem solving, etc.

6. To provide a joint experience between generations.

7. To help families discover and develop their strengths through increased loving, caring, joy, and creating.

8. To provide an opportunity for positive intervention into family systems so as to facilitate their living and growing together more productively.

When introducing the family cluster to the church or Sunday school, you will need to recognize this concept differs greatly from traditional modes of education within the church. It changes the structure of peer-oriented programs of Christian education. It emphasizes the systems approach to learning and change, as opposed to an individual approach within peer groups. This may mean reeducation of leaders and teachers and could also call for organizational changes as well.

I suggest you first consider a short-term pilot program without committing yourself to anything long-range. This approach will be less threatening and will help in setting future goals.

Recruit families who are active in the church and Sunday school with the idea that nonmember families will be included in succeeding clusters after you have trained several lead groups. Also, this may be an excellent way to return inactive families to the "mainstream" of Christian endeavor. New families would also benefit from the fellowship and sharing of established cluster groups.

Participating families will need to contract together and commit themselves as family units and individually to complete the time of training. Elements of a successful contract are found in chapter 3 of Margaret Sawin's *Family Enrichment With Family Clusters* (p. 44).

A suggested schedule for a 2-hour cluster session includes:

15 minutes	Presession activities
30 minutes	Light meal
20 minutes	Games, recreation, fun, singing
45 minutes	Structured educational experience on Bible-related theme
10 minutes	Evaluation and closure

Curriculum for cluster experiences can be found in the resources mentioned at the end of this book and in the subjects listed earlier for the Christian parenting class and the ministries described later in the chapter.

At the end of the unit of cluster sessions, an evaluation should be made through written remarks, questionnaires, verbal comments, etc. The purpose is to provide feedback for the participants and information for the Christian education director on how to plan for future projects.

When a cluster is reaching a termination point, it is vital to recognize the need for proper closure. Since parents and children have established emotional ties with members of the cluster through caring and sharing, the separation process must be a meaningful experience. The cluster will experience a "dying" time just as it experienced a beginning. Make this a time for Spirit-directed worship and *koinonia* sharing.

MARRIAGE-ENRICHMENT RETREAT

Another popular family-related ministry is marriage enrichment. Christian leaders should promote and support marriage enrichment now more than ever, not only because our culture is "down" on marriage and often it is the butt of jokes, but also because of Biblical incentives.

The marriage-enrichment retreat has great enrichment potential. It is an opportunity for interested couples, whatever their age or length of their marriage, to share their experiences with other couples and spend time alone. Couples are relieved when they find other couples have similar "growth pains" in their relationship and are also longing for enrichment.

Every marriage can be better, provided couples regularly invest in their relationship, interact with other Christian couples, get away for relaxation and worship, and educate themselves in enrichment techniques.

Couples need not be lectured to "death" at the retreat but should be actively involved from the very beginning in their own learning. Couples will get from the retreat only what they invest in it! A proven format suggests: couples receive instruction in small groups, break away for private couple discussions, then return to the group(s) for information sharing.

Keep promotion in a positive vein; the retreat is *not* a counseling event solely for couples having marital difficulties, but an *enrichment* experience designed to strengthen couple relationships.

All couples will not jump at the opportunity to attend, since many have their priorities out of order and allocate little time for personal and marital enrichment. Reason with the couples and encourage them to make a commitment to attend.

Make it clear that no one individual or couple will be pressured to share confidential marital information, but each person will be a voluntary participant in his own learning.

Emphasis should be placed on the Biblical basis of Christian marriage and how divine principles relate to each partner today. The primary need couples have is help in maintaining meaningful communication.

Additional subjects for discussion should include:

Marriage—Origin and need for enrichment
Foundations—Practical supports to a lasting, growing relationship
Roles—Compare perspectives of the other's role in marriage
Communication—Basic information and active listening exercise by partners

Conflict resolution—Practical, effective ways to deal with feelings (anger, fear); how to appropriate spiritual healing

Friday evening to Saturday afternoon is the more popular retreat format. However, concluding the retreat at Sunday noon gives the couples time to better comprehend the material and extends the enriching experience. Also, Sunday morning affords an excellent opportunity for worship, communion, and renewal of wedding vows.

The setting for a retreat need not be fancy. However, trying to house a seminar at the local church or in church members' homes has not proven successful. A nice motel in a nearby city could serve for the retreat when a more rustic setting is not available.

It is imperative that couples be able to retire in privacy after the evening sessions. Since many retreat facilities provide only dormitory-style housing, select a facility where couples can retreat to a place of their own for relaxation, intimacy, and rest. An alternative would be to have couples bring mobile homes, trailers, or campers to the retreat site.

This retreat is different from others in that the schedule is not filled with segregated group activities like volleyball, basketball, and unstructured time. It is a *couple* experience; it is structured to encourage couples to maximize their time *together*. There will be plenty of group interaction but the focus is on the couple's relationship.

Discussion Activities

1. Discuss the leader-couple idea suggested for the parenting class.

2. Discuss the basic differences between the family-enrichment seminar and family-enrichment leadership conference.

3. Discuss the philosophical distinctions between peer-oriented and clustering models of Christian education.

4. List the ways every marriage can be better.

5. What additional discovery groups could be included in the "Family Happening"?

10

Helping the Family
Face the Future

IN THIS CHAPTER RON MCMANUS, a Sunday school specialist, interviews the authors concerning the church and the family and how the two can face the future as a viable force.

Ron McManus: Gentlemen, how will the church meet the challenge of ministry to the family in the '80s?

Larry Summers: It will meet the challenge by understanding the meaning of enrichment. I think the church has put its emphasis on remedial ministry in the past—that is, trying to repair problems after they have occurred—rather than emphasizing prevention and enrichment. By prevention and enrichment, I mean doing something about problems before they happen and supporting the family's strengths and potential.

J. D. Middlebrook: I think in our society there is a feeling the family will not make it. Because of this, the church has the responsibility of emphasizing a Biblical family life. How this may be accomplished will depend on the individual situation. In a small town or rural area the challenge will not be the same as in a metropolitan, cosmopolitan locale. Each church will have to personalize its own challenge.

Ron McManus: What changes in basic family life-style do you think the '80s will bring?

J. D. Middlebrook: There are so many aspects of family life that to speak of them all at this point would be impossible, so I will just illustrate these changes. America is a mobile society; travel is part of our way of life. But with the energy and economic crises, we are going to be forced to reevaluate our life-style. This can be a blessing if it helps us develop a closeness and appreciation for our families.

The nuclear family is common in our society. But the extended family is important in the Christian community—even if "extended" means families outside of blood relationships. We may need to develop these relationships within the Christian community to add strength to our families.

Larry Summers: There is a trend for family life to be private and isolated, and this will probably continue. We've got to do something to offset this and bring families together in meaningful supportive relationships. We haven't dealt with this in the past, but we must in the future if we are to survive as a nation and as a culture.

Ron McManus: How can the church assist families in adjusting to these changes?

Larry Summers: The church must help the family understand true Christian values and show how to model these values and produce a Christian life-style in the home.

J. D. Middlebrook: This is true, but in the past I think we have been guilty of making the church or the school or some other institution responsible. For instance: "Look what the schools are doing to our children!" or, "The church has failed my child!" is often heard. I think we're going to have to realize the *family* is the most important socializing agent for ourselves and our children. If we can emphasize in our Christian education program that the family is primary, not secondary, then we will strengthen our families. We must emphasize this in our teaching, from the smallest child to the oldest member of our congregation.

Because of the energy crisis, the church is once again going to become the focus of life as it was in early America. Weekend trips may no longer be affordable for most families, and the church can provide a viable spiritual and social alternative. If the church takes advantage of this opportunity for ministry, these changes in American life-style can benefit both the church and the family.

Ron McManus: Pastor Middlebrook, in chapter 2 you said in the next decade "the Christian family will contrast more and more with the secular family." Could you elaborate on this?

J. D. Middlebrook: I will be happy to. In America, the family has always had the influence of the Christian church and the Christian religion. Our Judeo-Christian heritage has affected all of us. But as society has developed in the past decade, and continues to develop, there is less influence from these ideals and principles. Therefore, the Christian church and family will become more and more distinct from the rest of society. The standards, values, and beliefs of the Christian will stand in marked contrast to those of society.

I am certainly not calling for legalism. Legalism never contributes to the well-being of the Christian church or the family. But we must understand what the Scriptures teach a Christian is, and what a Christian family is. Then we must actualize this in our lives.

Ron McManus: What can the church do to unite rather than fragment the family? What can it do to help unite the family in ministry?

J. D. Middlebrook: I have always been concerned about not adding to a problem we're trying to solve. I believe our programming is going to have to become more focused. For example, you can't have something at the church every night of the week and expect the family battling energy and economic problems to get one member of the family there one night and another member there another night. So, we will have to simplify the programming of the church.

The fragmenting of the family hasn't been caused by deliberate efforts on the part of society. We have to realize the family itself has often willingly surrendered its responsibilities to various agencies. It may be necessary now for the family to assume responsibility for its children and its adults, rather than giving them to other agencies. So, the church can become the focal point of a united effort to bring families together.

Larry Summers: I fully agree. I see churches in the '80s involved in ministry *with* families rather than *for* families. Churches and families must do things together, rather than the church doing something for the family. In the past, we believed that through therapy and counseling we could solve the problems of the family, but now we need to emphasize the moral development of the strengths of the family and its members. We're talking about preventive as opposed to remedial ministries.

Ron McManus: We have been told that many people will

have more leisure time in the '80s. What can the church do to help families use this leisure time?

J. D. Middlebrook: I think it will depend on our concept of what a church is. If a church is only "a spiritual supplement to the family," then the important thing will be to have Bible studies and prayer meetings. But if the church has other duties, responsibilities, and roles, then it will be concerned with the well-being of its people's social life and provide recreational outlets for the family.

Another positive aspect of this increased leisure time is that members of the congregation can use their God-given talents and abilities in the ministry and life of the church.

Larry Summers: We must help family members establish Biblical priorities in their daily lives. When we become the models of Christian living that Christ wants us to be, the question of leisure will be taken care of.

Ron McManus: Larry, what do you feel is the church's responsibility to the family today?

Larry Summers: The church's chief responsibility to the family today is to enrich and support it. The church needs to reconfirm its commitment to these two things. Most families function at a very small fraction of their potential. The possibilities and potentialities of family living remain largely unexplored in our society and in the church.

Ron McManus: We've looked at the church's responsibility to the family. Pastor Middlebrook, what do you believe is the family's responsibility to the church?

J. D. Middlebrook: I think the family must understand that what it is, the church is. The church is not separated from and different from the family. The family *is* the church. It is this combination of many families that makes the church a viable body of believers.

In other words, my church will be what I am. If the family wants the church to be strong, then the family must be strong. If the family desires the church to have a ministry, then the family must have a ministry. The family must recommit itself to the importance of the church.

Ron McManus: Pastor Middlebrook, what suggestions do you have for fellow pastors regarding family ministry?

J. D. Middlebrook: As spiritual leaders, we must reemphasize the importance of the family in our own homes. We must love our children and our spouses. We must agree that the family is important to us. It doesn't matter what we say from the pulpit or in our programming, if it's not shown by what we do. We must begin to emphasize the family and encourage leadership in our churches. We must affirm the family by the way we live.

Ron McManus: Larry, if you could summarize for parents their family responsibilities, what would you share with them?

Larry Summers: We all resist changes in the family system, because we think we're doing okay and have no more problems than the next family. When you start talking about families, many parents get on a "guilt trip." But that's not the purpose of this book or of this emphasis in ministry. We must recognize the challenge before us and realize we can meet it. Family enrichment is not just for perfect parents; it's for all families. Parents must recognize their God-given responsibility and realign their priorities, with God first, their husband/wife second, and their family third. Then everything else will fall into place down the line.

Additional Resources

Gangel, Kenneth. *The Family First*. Minneapolis: HIS Publications.

Getz, Gene A. *The Measure of a Family*. Glendale, CA: Gospel Light/ Regal Books, 1976.

Howell, John C. *Senior Adult Family Life*. Nashville: Broadman Press, 1979.

Hutka, Ed. *Boom or Busted?* Plainfield, NJ: Logos International, 1979.

Kerr, Horace. *How to Minister to Senior Adults*. Nashville: Broadman Press, 1980.

Mace, Dave and Vera. *How to Have a Happy Marriage*. Nashville: Abingdon Press, 1977.

Mains, Karen. *Open Heart–Open Home*. Elgin, IL: David C. Cook Pub. Co., 1976.

Osborne, Cecil. *The Art of Understanding Your Mate*. Grand Rapids: Zondervan Publishing House, 1970.

Petri, Darlene. *The Hurt and Healing of Divorce*. Elgin, IL: David C. Cook Publishing Co., 1976.

Rickerson, Wayne E. *Getting Your Family Together*. Glendale, CA: Gospel Light/Regal Books, 1977.

_____. *How to Help the Christian Home*. Glendale, CA: Gospel Light/Regal Books.

Sloane, Valerie. *Creative Family Activities*. Nashville: Abingdon Press, 1976.

Smoke, Jim. *Growing Through Divorce*. Irvine, CA: Harvest House Publishers, 1976.

Vigeveno, H. S., and Anne Claire. *Divorce and the Children*. Glendale, CA: Gospel Light/Regal Books, 1979.

Wagner, Peter. *Your Spiritual Gifts*. Glendale, CA: Gospel Light/ Regal Books, 1979.

Wakefield, Norm. *A Happier Family*. Glendale, CA: Gospel Light/ Regal Books.

Wheat, Ed and Gaye. *Intended for Pleasure.* Old Tappan, NJ: Fleming H. Revell, 1977.

Whitehouse, Donald and Nancy. *Pray and Play.* Nashville: Broadman Press, 1979.

Wood, Britton. *Single Adults Want to Be the Church, Too.* Nashville: Broadman Press, 1977.

Wright, H. Norman. *Communication: Key to Your Marriage.* Glendale, CA: Gospel Light/Regal Books, 1974.

Packets and Periodicals

Family Life Today. Gospel Light Publications, 110 W. Broadway, Glendale, CA 91204.

Family Ministry Packet. Gospel Publishing House, 1445 Boonville, Springfield, MO 65802. (Order no. 08-0606, $19.95.)

God's Word for Today. Gospel Publishing House. (Subscription $2.80 per year; $2.60 in bundle of two or more; individual copies 60¢ each. Published quarterly.)

Higher Goals for Your Family Packet. Gospel Publishing House. (Order no. 08-0607, $3.00.)